THE SINGER'S HANDBOOK
A GUIDE FOR ASPIRING SINGERS

Contents

Mary King

Mary King is a highly experienced performer, creative director and vocal coach. A distinguished interpreter, she has made a particular feature of contemporary repertoire and has appeared in many roles on the operatic stage, working with many conductors and orchestras across the world including Oliver Knussen and Sir Simon Rattle, the Berlin Philharmonic, the Cleveland and Concertgebouw Orchestras. She has regularly performed works such as *Pierrot Lunaire*, *Where The Wild Things Are*, Ligeti's *Aventures* and *Nouvelles Aventures*, and sung many operatic roles including Marcellina (*Nozze Di Figaro*), Baba the Turk (*Rake's Progress*), Cockerel (*Cunning Little Vixen*), Mrs Goose (*Turn of the Screw*) and Meg Page (*Falstaff*).

Mary was Artistic Associate of English National Opera's Baylis Programme from 2004-2006 and during her long association with the company she ran ENO's highly successful performance skills course, 'The Knack' for eleven years.

In November 2006, Mary was appointed Head of the new Southbank Centre Voicelab. From casting for professional projects, creating a core ensemble from diverse backgrounds (as well as a series of larger associate ensembles), to encouraging vocal talent in all forms, Mary is at the heart of vocal activity at the Southbank Centre.

Mary King is increasingly widely known through her work on television and was one of the driving forces behind Channel 4's critically acclaimed and award winning *Operatunity*, a five week television series introducing opera to the wider public. This was followed by *Musicality*, also on Channel 4, a five part series on music theatre and in July 2006 she was the expert analyst at Cardiff Singer of the World for BBC Television.

Anthony Legge

Anthony Legge studied at the Guildhall, Oxford University and the London Opera Centre, and also studied accompanying privately with Geoffrey Parsons and Paul Hamburger. His numerous recitals include those with, amongst others, Dame Janet Baker, Sir Thomas Allen, Gwynne Howell and Håkan Hagegård. He has worked regularly with the principal British opera companies, Glyndebourne Festival Opera, Opera Australia, many European opera companies and at Bayreuth, where he assisted on the Kupfer-Barenboim Ring cycle for five years and a new production of *Die Meistersinger*. He has been Head of Music at English National Opera for 14 years where he conducted performances of *Dido And Aeneas*, *Orpheus And Eurydice*, *Lulu* and *Alcina*.

Anthony is Music Director of Clonter Opera where he has conducted *Butterfly*, *Wienerblut* and *La Traviata*. He is also Music Director of the Mastersingers Company, which encourages young Wagnerian singers and for them has conducted *Rheingold*, *Walküre Act III* and *Siegfried Act III,* and *Götterdämmerung* with the Rehearsal Orchestra. He conducted the final orchestra concert at the Spitalfields Festival in London in 2005. Anthony has worked on much contemporary music and Wagner with the BBC Symphony Orchestra. He works regularly for the Nederlandsche Oper in Amsterdam and is a frequent visiting vocal coach for the Royal Opera House Young Singers Programme and Opera Australia.

Currently, Anthony is Director of Opera at the Royal Academy of Music and Music Advisor to Grange Park Opera. He has recorded two CDs with Chandos accompanying Linda Finnie, and has a book published by Peters Edition entitled *The Art of Auditioning*. Anthony also appeared as a judge on the Channel 4 *Operatunity* series.

Introduction

Singing is a wonderful thing!

It can be done by almost everyone, make you feel good inside and improve your health. It can enrich your life by enabling you to experience music from the inside. Vocal music can be enjoyed at many different levels: there are many non-professional choirs, operatic societies, festivals and competitions and they are available to every age group and musical persuasion.

Every singer is unique. Each person has a mouth, a tongue, a throat, a vocal mechanism, a neck, a set of lungs, and so on but there are subtle differences in the ways that these common features are assembled. The *differences* are more important than the *similarities*. Different body, different sensibility, different personality equals different – and unique – voice.

Whilst many people can sing *well*, few people can earn their living from it; furthermore, only a very few of those who can sing professionally are going to be world-class household names. You may begin aiming at a professional musical life but decide after some time that it is not the life for you. Conversely, you may take a degree, which leads you to a career unrelated to music and then decide later that you want to head for the professional musical market instead. Assuming you are hopeful of having a professional life, then you could aim to work in a big 'pond' – a national or international company – though you will almost certainly begin in a smaller 'pond'. What determines which of these will suit you is a complex arrangement of attributes and skills, including:

- Vocal quality and size, vocal range, stamina, general health, musicianship, application, concentration, graft, looks, charisma, acting skill, communication, temperament, sociability.
- The ability to take on information and process it, to multi-task, to collaborate with others, to network.
- The passion to continue, whatever disappointments come your way.
- Luck, or being in the right place at the right time.

Some of these qualities you will have naturally; some you will be able to acquire; some may elude you.

We hope in this book to be able to point you in the right direction: to open a window onto the world of music and singing, so that you can become better informed and more in control of your own development. We hope that through the information in this book *any* singer – professional, aspiring professional or amateur enthusiast – will find tools to develop their talents.

Between the two of us, we have had much experience in the musical and singing world, and this book is the fruit of that experience. Of course, it is also true that there are many, many other people who *also* have much experience, which will differ from ours. Using this book as a starting point, we hope that you will have many interesting discussions with your teachers and colleagues on the topics that follow. There is information about what usually happens at each of the different stages of a singer's development; there are some handy tips based on our teaching experience; there are practical things for you to try.

There are many 'rules' in singing and when you start you may feel besieged by them! However, they are not fixed in stone. Your voice will carry on changing and developing for as long as you sing. So, whatever your training and tuition, the most important thing of all is that you learn to make your voice *uniquely yours*.

Whichever your path, singing should be pleasurable for you and for your audiences. What we hope above all is that you enjoy singing the wonderful vocal music that awaits you.

Mary King and Anthony Legge

Key to symbols used in this book:

❗   Useful advice/ hint

♪   Take note

📖   Glossary/ dictionary term

☆   Anecdote

🏋   Exercise to try

💡   Idea

© 2007 by Faber Music Ltd
First published by Faber Music Ltd in 2007
3 Queen Square, London WC1N 3AU

Designed by Sue Clarke

Printed in England by Caligraving Ltd
All rights reserved

ISBN10: 0-571-52720-5
EAN13: 978-0-571-52720-5

To buy Faber Music publications or to find out about the full range of titles available,
please contact your local music retailer or Faber Music sales enquiries:

Faber Music Ltd, Burnt Mill, Elizabeth Way, Harlow, CM20 2HX England
Tel: +44(0)1279 82 89 82 Fax: +44(0)1279 82 89 83
sales@fabermusic.com fabermusic.com

1 On your starting blocks

In this section of the book, we will concentrate on:
- The singing teacher.
- How the voice works and some basic anatomy.
- Vocal hygiene.
- How to warm-up and practise.

The singing teacher

The first thing that a prospective singer has to do is to find a teacher who will be able to give them a good solid technical grounding. In the first months of your work, you will have to trust your teacher to guide you in almost everything that you do. They will advise you on many things: suitable repertoire, vocal exercises, how, when and where to practise, and so on. They may also recommend other related professionals whom you might need. For example, they may have a regular pianist who they know will be able to teach you the notes of a song and make suggestions that are in line with their own technical objectives for you. They might even suggest some supportive physical work to help you develop – Alexander technique, yoga, pilates or Feldenkrais, for instance.

As a budding singer, you are an athlete. Like an athlete, you will have to become very 'body-aware'. This is nothing to do with body fascism or 'the body beautiful' but only to do with understanding that your voice is MORE than the small mechanism that you feel in your throat. Think of your *whole body* as scaffolding around the small and intricate building that is your vocal mechanism. You must remember that your voice is going to be put under pressure if you do not allow the larger muscles of the body to support the smaller ones. There are many factors to consider when learning how to sing. You will need to learn how to co-ordinate all the relevant muscles of your body. It may be that you find some things easy, others much harder.

The singing teacher will begin by working on the fundamentals of vocal technique, which are:

- How to breathe effectively.
- How to keep the throat open at all times.
- How to make a clear tone across the entire vocal range.
- How to project tone and volume without undue effort and pressure.
- How to activate the muscles used in singing to support your sound.

They will then go on to suggest and work on pieces of repertoire appropriate to your voice type and level of ability. Through these pieces, they will develop your musical and interpretative skills, so that you learn to use your technical craft for expressive purpose.

How do you find a teacher?

Finding the right teacher for you is a bit like finding a lifetime partner – what suits one person may not suit another! You may have to have more than one go at finding the right person and it is important to bear in mind the following:

- Try to find your teacher through personal recommendation, rather than responding to adverts.
- Talk to other singers about their teachers but be aware that it is not always

the case that the best singer you hear has the best teacher.

- Teachers are human beings! You may find that you have a personality clash that will get in the way of your learning.
- You must give a reasonable time to each teacher that you have – there is no such thing as a quick fix in singing and certainly not at the beginning of your vocal training.
- Every good teacher can teach you something. No one person has *all* of the answers.
- The teacher's job is to *guide* the pupil through dependency to self-sufficiency. No teacher can wave a magic wand – you have to do your bit too. Before you reject a teacher as ineffective, you have to be sure you're doing what they have asked (with regard to practice, repertoire, vocal hygiene, and so on).

Once you have chosen your teacher

You will usually have a regular lesson. This is so that you can take on information *gradually*. Most beginners will have one lesson a week of an hour each time. Sometimes, they will have more frequent and slightly shorter lessons. Your teacher will guide you in what they think is most appropriate for you. Regular lessons help you to get into reliable habits. It is certainly not good to practise on your own without understanding what you are doing – it is very hard to correct ingrained bad habits!

As your understanding of your own voice develops, you also develop surer methods of evaluating your progress. At first you have to trust your teacher, who is experiencing your voice in the way that an audience will. What you hear and feel inside your body as your sound may not be the same as the sound that the listener hears. Matching these two 'truths' may take years. Progress in singing comes from not merely understanding intellectually what the teacher is asking for but being able to register and reproduce the physical sensations associated with good singing.

Teachers should develop confidence in their pupils. Success in singing is bound up with confidence. When you perform you must put your technical strivings aside and concentrate on the pleasure of singing and performing.

As your confidence increases, you will feel able to ask questions. You may need to negotiate a way of doing this effectively. Sometimes a question, which you intend to be about clarification of an instruction, may come across to the teacher as unwillingness to try something. If you *question verbally* more frequently than you *explore vocally*, you may hold up the learning process. Try first, question later!

You will need to learn how to accept criticism, without it undermining your confidence. You also need to learn how to accept a compliment, if you yourself have not been pleased by something you have done.

Advanced study

Advanced study demands an ever-increasing attention spent on the smallest of details. The better you get, the harder it is to increase your skill. Advanced study also implies that for the most part, you are able to look after yourself when rehearsing a production. Your lessons then may become more of a troubleshooting affair. As you become more accomplished, lessons become less frequent and could be taken in concentrated spells.

Remember that voices change as they develop. You will need to make adjustments as time goes on. You may have exaggerated one aspect of your technique at the expense of another.

At some time, you may need to change your teacher. Sometimes a new teacher will see you as a 'blank page' and this can be refreshing and stimulating.

It is quite usual to have lessons for the entire duration of your singing career. As you acquire more skill and a fine reputation, your teacher becomes a trusted colleague who will give honest and impartial advice.

Methods of teaching singing

There are many methods of teaching and learning. Some of the methods used for teaching singing are scientific, involving analysis of the anatomy of the vocal mechanism and all relevant muscles; some revolve around the use of imagery. The method of teaching that helps the individual singer is often determined by the way that a pupil learns best – some are happier identifying sensation through their imagination and others prefer a more scientific approach. Whatever the method, the student needs to be able to reproduce the sensation of good singing and will need to develop great physical awareness.

♪ ALL teaching is a combination of the work that the teacher does and the work that the pupil does.

As the vocal mechanism is *inside* your body, it is difficult to be certain of what you are doing, physically, all the time. A teacher gives you constant feedback from the *outside*.

A typical singing lesson

Most lessons involve many exchanges between teacher and pupil. They may be verbal exchanges, or they might involve vocal demonstration and imitation. Information about what to do, why it is happening, how you feel, and so on, is constantly being given, refined and even contradicted! You will need to be patient. You will also find that trying too hard to do all the things that you are being asked to do may get in the way of accomplishing these things successfully. You may also get frustrated by the fact that you *understand intellectually* what you are being asked to do but you cannot *do it physically*.

Usually, you will be required to try a vocal exercise and then it will be assessed, both by you and the teacher. You may be asked: 'How did it feel?', 'What did it sound like to your ear?', 'Can you make the same sound again?'.

You will be bombarded with information and sensation. You will find that you have to learn how to understand your vocal equipment. You never know how your voice sounds once it leaves your mouth. You must learn to trust another person's ears.

Terminology

In this section, we will introduce you to some of the terms you might hear in your lessons. Each teacher is likely to have a slightly different way of phrasing things, so if it is not clear, you must always ask.

Posture

Although many singing teachers talk about *relaxation*, be aware that singing is an athletic activity for which you need to train your muscles. Perhaps it is better to assume that you must have an *absence of tension*, rather than be truly relaxed. Singing will involve muscular tension *and* relaxation.

The way you hold yourself can have a direct connection to the quality of your voice. The spine should be aligned correctly, without an exaggerated curve in either the small of the back or around the neck. The knees should be soft and not 'locked back' as this will affect your breathing. Experiment with where you naturally hold your weight. Do you want to go forward or back? Do you use your shoulders to make yourself appear straight? Your centre of gravity should feel quite low.

To develop a greater awareness of your body, try the following:

> When standing, place your shoulders, hips, knees and feet in a straight line. Keep your neck long so that your head is equally balanced both side-to-side (ear to ear) and front-to-back (neither pulled too far back making you double chinned, nor with your chin protruding making you resemble a chicken). Keep the pelvis slightly forward and your knees slightly bent. Keep your shoulders relaxed. Now, 'swing' the body rotating from the waist or hips.
>
> Lie on the floor, on your back with your knees up and your head supported by a book. You should feel your whole spine in contact with the floor.
>
> Stand up with your back against a door or wall. Keep your feet a few inches away from the door/wall. With your shoulders low and knees slightly bent, keep contact with the door or wall from the crown of your head to the base of your spine. You may have to change the angle of your pelvis. Find a position that is comfortable.

Breathing and airflow

You need more air for singing than for everyday talking. You need to maximise the amount of air you breathe in and then be able to control the way that you breathe out. This is sometimes called **breath control** or **breath management**.

In speech, we take air as we need, often snatching it. Most people breathe very shallowly. A singer has to learn to breathe much lower than is necessary in everyday life. A singer has to learn to use the **lower abdominal muscles**, situated above the pubic bone. By relaxing these lower muscles, the diaphragm can drop down. This creates the maximum available space in the lungs. When the diaphragm is held high, the lung capacity is much smaller.

When you take a breath, you will feel the ribs expand at your sides and at your back. Your ribs should NOT lift up at the front of your chest and your shoulders should remain low. You should also be aware of the necessity of a *silent* breath.

Some singers inhale very noisily – sometimes through the mouth and sometimes through the nose. You must aim to make your breathing inaudible as well as effective.

As you breathe *out*, you will need to keep your torso as expanded as you can. Your **intercostal muscles** will keep the ribs wide. However, this does not mean that you HOLD the abdominal wall at the front of the body rigid. As the breath comes out, you will feel the lower abdominal muscles contract. If you hold your breath on empty (that is, let go of all your air and then hold it) you will discover a reflex action, whereby the lower abdominal muscles expand again, thus allowing the diaphragm to drop. You will be able to make this a natural and automatic physical action. **Do not collapse the whole chest!**

It is important to be aware of the way you release the out-breath – the **airflow** must be constant, there must not be 'bulges' in the flow of the air. Also, and most importantly, you must be able to control the **pressure** of this air. If the pressure is too high, then you will feel tension in your torso. Think of the difference between blowing out a candle gently and blowing up a balloon. The first action will have lower breath pressure than the second. Be sure that you do not hold on to the air – it must flow. Breath conservation is not breath control or management!

A singer learns to control air from the abdominal muscles, rather than 'snatching' air with the mouth. The **thorax** – the part of the body enclosed by the ribs – remains stable, whether breath is being inhaled or exhaled.

Young singers often 'drive' or 'push' the air. They sometimes think that this is what constitutes a 'free' sound or 'letting go'. If you drive air persistently, then you risk vocal damage. Your vocal folds are delicate; they do not cope well with extremes of air passing through them.

In musical theatre, rock and pop, all of the above applies *except in 'belting'*. This quality of sound will demand that you take a higher breath, with more tension in the upper body. The sound is an exciting one essential to much of the modern musical theatre repertoire. If you do not find it comes naturally, then you will need to be coached in how to make the sound safely and in a way that does not tire you, harm your instrument or reduce your ability to make a whole array of vocal sounds. Remember that belting is only one vocal colour and should not be used all the time!

Try the following:

> Put your hands on your lower abdominal muscles. In this position, release all your air in a long 'sss' sound. As you do this, your abdominal muscles will contract – a bit like trying on a pair of trousers with a zip that are a little too tight.
>
> Hold your breath on 'empty'. When you are REALLY ready for air, take a breath and notice your abdominal muscles releasing, and expanding outwards. Let your air out again on an 'sss' sound, as slowly and evenly as you can – with no blurting out of air. Keep your neck relaxed (but not floppy) and your throat open. Do not collapse the chest!

If you find it hard to feel the muscles moving in your back, bend over the back of a chair when doing your breathing exercises – it is often easier to feel what's going on.

Making sound

The larynx

The primary function of the **larynx** is to stop food going down the airway into the lungs. When we swallow, the breath is held and the valve that is the larynx closes over – thus protecting the airways from foreign matter – and food goes down the gullet into the stomach; if food goes down the wrong way, we cough violently in order to expel it. As singers, we are more interested in the larynx's function in making sound.

The larynx is an extraordinarily complex mechanism, situated just behind your Adam's apple. It can move up and down. If you make as if to swallow, you will feel it rise up; if you complete the swallowing action, you will feel it go back down again. If you yawn, you will feel it go even lower.

The Western classical music aesthetic demands a low position for the larynx. This is thought to maximise the depth and richness of the vocal sound. You may have to learn to lower your larynx – but be conscious that there is a difference between a low larynx position, which is natural and free (even if acquired through extensive training), and that which is forced. The forced position involves pressing the back of the tongue to hold the larynx down. This produces a sound with a damped or covered quality, without brightness, and frequently with impaired facility for top notes. In musical theatre you may well have to use a neutral larynx position to make a more natural sound. For safe belting, the larynx will be high and not low.

The vocal folds

These are held in place by a complex arrangement of cartilage and muscle. The **vocal folds** (used to be known as 'cords') are actually the *edges* of the **vocalis muscle** and it is these edges that vibrate together. The speed at which these folds vibrate determines the pitch of the sound. They are able to change length and also to change mass (that is, be thick or thin). The longer the folds, the higher the pitch; the shorter they are, the lower the pitch. Thicker vocal folds are associated with louder and fuller sounds, often easier to make in the middle or bottom of a singers' range (depending of course on voice type). Thinner folds are required for quiet or *mezza di voce* sounds.

When you breathe, the space between the two edges is wide open. When you make sound – either in speech or song – the air comes from your lungs into the **trachea** (windpipe) and gradually up the tube until it reaches the larynx, and the vocal folds within. With the air coming up from underneath, the vocal folds begin to vibrate and in so doing they make sound. As you make a sound, you aim to have the edges of the folds adducting together along their whole length. If the sound you make is very breathy, it may mean that there is a gap between the folds that is not closing properly. You will need to attend to this, as prolonged use of non-adducted folds can lead to vocal problems. Try this:

*Make the sound 'ng' (as in the word 'singing'). Make sure that you are making a true 'ng' and not an 'n'. Slide up and down your whole range, effortlessly gliding between the different **registers** of your voice. Make sure you do not grip your throat to force the sound out. If you find difficulty between registers and you 'clunk' from one to the other, slide slower until you can achieve a true glide.*

Support

With all sound, it is necessary to engage the muscles of support, which include many of the larger muscular structures in the body. All singing teachers talk about support. It is essential that you learn the physical sensations associated with a supported sound. An unsupported sound will not 'travel' and will encourage you to force your voice.

Push your hands into the sides of your waist, so that there is some resistance to them. Make a small cough. You should feel an instantaneous muscular kick against your hands. If you make a rolled 'rr' sound, you will also feel this expansion and you will also notice an engagement of muscular activity around the lower abdominal area and the back. You will also feel a kick at the top of the ribs and just above your collarbone. Sing some small scales, concentrating on feeling this muscular activity. Don't force it!

Initiating a note

There are several ways that you can initiate sound. The start of a note is often called the **onset**. There are three kinds:

Aspirate

Start exhaling on an 'h' and then gradually begin to make that 'h' turn to sound. This is called an aspirated attack.

In classical singing, the aspirate mustn't be too intrusive, as you are aiming for something 'purer'. In pop or musical theatre you may use this sound a lot. The use of a microphone enables you to achieve an intimate connection without great projection. Microphones tend to 'like' breathy singing and find focussed and projected sounds harder to deal with.

Glottal

The glottal stop (or glottal plosive/glottal shock) occurs when the two sides of the vocal folds are shut tight with air pressure building up underneath. When the sound is made there is a 'pop' or 'click' as the sound is released. It is used as an effect for emphasis in classical singing but *rarely very strongly*. It is an essential part of a musical theatre singers' technique.

If you find this hard to produce, then try:

- *Making the sound of an automatic rifle 'uh-uh-uh-uh' in quick fire.*
- *Making the sound associated with a slang meaning of 'oh dear' or 'something's up' – 'uh-oh'.*

Whatever the style of music you are singing, you should learn to make the glottal cleanly and efficiently. Don't make it your only method of starting a note. Over-emphasis of the glottal is not to be encouraged.

Simultaneous or co-ordinated

The desired onset in classical singing is the one that can barely be heard – where the air making the vibration is efficiently co-ordinated with the beginning of the sound. See if you can start a sound on a vowel, with neither aspirate or glottal at the front of it. Remember to keep the in-breath inaudible!

The onset of a note is important, as it will affect the pressure at which air is coming across your folds. You must maintain easy and even airflow if you are to achieve good legato singing and evenness of sound.

Ending a note

Just as you aimed to start a note imperceptibly, so you should be able to end it. Make sure there is no collapse of the chest and ribs at the end of a phrase or breath. Make sure there is no 'click' from the vocal folds after the end of the note. This means you are controlling the airflow by closing your folds together, rather than by abdominal means. Check that you have not finished the note by 'damping' the sound, either by pressing the tongue root down your throat, or gripping your throat muscles, or even by closing your mouth or jaw.

Registers and resonance

As the melody goes along you will of course change pitch. In doing so, you may encounter vocal 'turbulence' as you change **registers**. Although there are changing fashions in vocal terminology, you may well find this term in common use. There are different sounds in your voice according to where you are in your range. They have been defined as 'head' and 'chest' tones. The head sounds are the sounds, usually higher in pitch, of sweet sounding 'pure' tones, whereas the chest sounds are the lower and more 'earthy' registers. Whatever the terminology your teacher uses, it is undoubtedly the case that a complex muscular manoeuvre is occurring when you change from one kind of tone to another. For good singing, you will need to be able to maintain colour and quality across registers. Contradictorily, you can also emphasise the difference between these two sorts if the dramatic intention requires such emphasis.

Resonance is also a frequently used term and can mean that the sound 'rings', or can be more precisely applied to where you feel the sound vibrating. In fact, any place where the sound 'hangs around' after being made can act as a resonator. You can thus have **nasal resonance** (not always desirable!), **chest resonance** and it also occurs in many places around the head and neck. The teacher is always trying to get these resonances balanced and make sure that you are not using one at the expense of another. A resonant sound is the sound that projects.

Try:

- *Making a lowish hum on 'mmm' and put your hands on your body where you feel the sensation of buzzing. Change pitch and see if the sensation moves.*
- *Join the 'mmm' to a vowel and try to maintain the same buzzing.*

Many teachers spend much time over the **passaggio**. This is the area of pitch that acts as a 'bridge' between your registers. In other words, where you can make both sorts of sound but have to negotiate exactly how you will change gear. You may have problems negotiating both a lower 'bridge' and a higher one. For most voices, these notes are around E♭ or F in both octaves.

Another frequently used term is the vocal **mix**. This describes the sound at the lower end of the voice, where it is possible to add more head sound to the chest sound. You should also be aware of the term **tessitura**. Literally, this means weaving and describes the area of pitch that any given piece of music occupies. Thus a piece may have a top C but not have a particularly high tessitura if the top C occurs only once and the general pitch of the piece is much lower. A piece with constantly high tessitura could be one where the vocal line is persistently around G or A but never goes to a high C. In musical theatre there is a tendency to overuse the chest sounds and take them too high in the voice. You should be able to siren effortlessly between your registers without aggressive gear changes.

The **countertenor** voice is a bit of a special case. The modern male alto does not sing in his 'modal' or speech voice range; he uses a 'falsetto' and controls this sound with great skill. In this voice type, the vocal folds are meeting along a very thin edge and not – initially – vibrating much at all. Countertenors need to learn to blend the falsetto range as it meets the modal range. In many cases these singers are imitating the voices of the 'castrati' – the male singers of the seventeenth and eighteenth centuries, who were castrated in order to preserve their boyhood vocal ranges, some of the best of which became superstars. Modern day countertenors have become very skilled and much in demand.

The throat

The throat, that is to say the **pharyngeal tube**, should be open at all times. There are many ways of getting this feeling, which is one of the fundamentals of singing. When your throat is relaxed, or at least is free from tension (which is not quite the same thing), singing feels easy – indeed, effortless. You should have a feeling in the throat as if you are about to laugh or try to imagine the excited feeling you had as a child when looking forward to presents on Christmas day! You need to make sure that you are not squeezing the sound – it may sound very focussed to you but to others it sounds forced and tight.

Jaw, tongue and mouth

The jaw

In order to have maximum space in the mouth for the sound to resonate in, you will need to learn to relax your jaw. Modern life brings with it many frustrations and anxieties, and tension will often be directly located in your jaw.

The jaw should be relaxed at the **temporomandibular joint** (the big hinge which allows you to open your mouth wide). There should be a wide space inside the back of your mouth – can you put one or two fingers between your top and bottom back molars? You may have to extend the space gradually. Make sure that you haven't thrust the jaw *forward* before dropping it. It should feel as if it is 'hanging' open. You should be able to articulate most consonants and vowels with your jaw uniformly open – don't shut the mouth to change vowels.

The tongue

The tongue must be very flexible. The tip, blade and back of the tongue have much work to do, forming clear and distinct vowels as well as precise and correctly placed consonants.

There is also the **tongue root**, which you can feel from the exterior by putting your hand on your throat right up under your chin (if you yawn, you will feel something pressing downwards – this is the root of your tongue). The root should not be employed in forcibly *holding down* the larynx: you will need to find a way of maintaining the lower larynx position without over-using this muscle. Neither should it be over-employed when you change pitch. If you sing an arpeggio, the notes should not be 'marked' by tongue root movements. You can *feel* this with your hand placed (gently!) round your throat; you can also *hear* the difference in tone – if your tongue is overworking, then the sound will bulge as you go from note to note.

To exercise the tip of the tongue, try:
- *Rolling the tip on a 'rr' sound.*
- *Rolling the back on a French or guttural 'rr'.*
- *Rolling the two together, making both sounds at once.*

To exercise the back of the tongue:
- *Place the tip of your tongue behind your bottom teeth. Without moving the tip, and with your mouth open and not moving your jaw, move the back of your tongue forwards and backwards. Do this in a mirror, until you are familiar with the feeling of this isolated muscular exercise.*

To eliminate overuse of the tongue root:
- *Practise scales and arpeggios with your tongue sticking out of your mouth!*

The soft palate

The soft palate is situated in the roof of your mouth. If you trace the roof of your mouth with the tip of your tongue from the front to the back you will feel:

- First: the teeth and behind them a ridge – the **alveolar ridge**.
- Then: a dome-like shape – the **hard palate**.
- Next: a softer tissue – the **soft palate**.
- Lastly: behind all that, the little flap of tissue hanging down – the **uvula**.

When you take a sharp intake of breath – in fear or excitement for example – you will feel the soft palate rising. You can get the same sensation by yawning, or by breathing in intensely ('smelling a rose') through the nose. The soft palate must be raised to give a gleam to your sound. Make sure that you can raise the soft palate without depressing the tongue root.

Vibrato

The preferred sound in Western classical singing has **vibrato** or variation in vibration; this vibration should be consistent throughout the range and whatever the volume. From singer to singer, there may be variation in the speed of the vibrato. If it becomes VERY slow, then it is usually called a **wobble** and if it is very fast it is called a **flutter**. Neither of these extremes is thought desirable! Many other forms of singing do not have vibrato – in early music or musical theatre, for example, it will be inserted as an expressive and emotional tool rather than the norm, and you must be able to control it.

Scientists do not agree as to how vibrato is made but it seems to be a combination of laryngeal and breath movements. It is not made by pushing an excess of air, or by manoeuvring the jaw up and down very fast!

The singing teacher and the use of imagery

Because your vocal apparatus is inside you, it is very difficult to be really clear about all technical matters. A student pianist can be told how to hold his or her arms or fingers, and so on, because every action of playing is observable. A singing teacher may concentrate on using words and images to help you find sensations within you. For example, they might compare a ball balanced on a fountain of water with the sensation of spinning a vocal sound on a fountain of air. These descriptions will of course differ from teacher to teacher, as each teacher uses their own language and imagery.

Vocal hygiene

Vocal health is the most important thing in a singer's life. If you start your singing life with a good regime, then you will get the most out of your voice. Here are some basic principles:

- Keep hydrated. Many of the most common health problems for singers have to do with being dehydrated:
  - You want to flush through any germs.
  - You need to keep the protective mucus in the larynx thin. The thicker it is, the more likely it is to clog around the folds, which will prevent them vibrating properly and may encourage you to force to get your sound out.
  - Increase your intake of fluid gradually to a total of around two or three litres a day. Sip rather than gulp – don't drink the day's quota in one go!
  - Coffee, tea and alcohol all dehydrate the voice, so keep these to a minimum and drink water alongside them.
- Avoid eating any one food type in excess. Learn to listen to your own body and what food it likes. Some foods may not be good for you. If you suffer from too much mucus, you could try cutting out dairy and yeast products.
- Avoid eating late at night, especially spicy foods. Leave at least two hours between finishing a meal and bedtime. Late night eating increases the risk of acid reflux[1].
- Avoid smoky, airless places whenever possible. This may actually mean: avoid smoking! All smoke, whether in the form of nicotine or more 'recreational' substances, is an irritant to the throat and also increases acid reflux.
- Avoid speaking or shouting amidst loud ambient noise – in a pub, club or inside a car, for example.
- Try to avoid long telephone calls, which might encourage prolonged and poor vocal production. A part-time job in telesales is not a good idea for a singer!
- If you are asthmatic, make sure you have the most effective inhalers. There is evidence that long-term use of steroid inhalers can produce or exacerbate vocal problems.

1 Acid reflux is a condition where the stomach acids come back up through the vocal tract and attack the vocal folds. It brings extreme discomfort and a burning sensation.

What to do if you get sick

- Steam: put your head over a bowl of boiling/very hot water and cover your head with a towel. You should do this 10 minutes at a time, several times a day. Don't always put proprietary decongestants in the water, as they may irritate the delicate vocal mechanism. Hot showers are also a good method of inhaling steam.
- Gargle with warm salt water, or a solution of warm water and bicarbonate of soda, to alleviate soreness and cleanse the throat. **DO NOT GARGLE WITH ASPIRIN** as there is a risk of haemorrhaging in the vocal folds.
- Take hot and cold drinks alternately – this can work effectively, rather in the same way as hot and cold compresses on the outer body.
- Boost your immune system – garlic, vitamin C, zinc and echinacea can all be helpful.
- Don't rush from the warm into the cold outside without effective protection in the form of clothing!

Coughs and colds

Some people fight infections more effectively than others. Keeping generally healthy is obviously sensible but there is no point in being over-precious. A professional singer needs to be able to perform very well, even when under the weather. You will learn with experience when you should cancel a performance and when you should carry on. It may be that being under par will only show as a *slight* diminution of skill and will not be ruinous to the performance as a whole. Whether you cancel may have to do more with what you are expected to sing. When your throat is sore – before a cold for example – it is better not to sing. Once the cold has come out, there is no reason not to sing and the voice may not be hampered much at all.

Try to avoid coughing. Prolonged coughing will definitely impair your vocal equipment. For temporary conditions, you may find honey and lemon (liquid or pastilles) soothing and you can also buy glycerine (liquid) on its own. If you have a persistent cough, you may need to seek medical help. It may indicate other conditions – perhaps asthma, for example.

Laryngitis

Laryngitis is an inflammatory condition that means that the vocal folds will not function properly. You will not be able to make a clear siren if you have laryngitis – the sound simply will not come out. With this condition, you should not attempt to sing. In fact, **DO NOT SPEAK**. Particularly, **DO NOT WHISPER**. Your voice will come back much more quickly if you give it complete rest and whispering is harder on the vocal folds than anything else.

Persistent hoarseness, breathiness, loss of voice or vocal impairment

It may be that for a mixture of reasons you experience a diminution of vocal quality, which cannot be explained as the consequence of a common cold or virus. You may become hoarse or feel that your usual vocal quality is impaired and no longer has the range or power that is normal to you. You will need to find the root cause and there are several common medical ones:

- You may have a problem with acid reflux.
- You may have a polyp, cyst or nodule – all three are variants of small growths on the vocal folds, made of soft or hard tissue.
- You may have tonsils that need to come out because they are causing repeated infections.
- You may suffer from allergic reactions – these can vary from fabric (perhaps on a costume) to certain foods.

If these are the problems, then you may be referred to a consultant laryngologist, who will examine your throat with specialist equipment in order to determine the best course of action. You may be referred to a speech therapist or osteopath, or – in the case of acid reflux – simple medication may be the answer. Surgery (to remove nodules/cysts and so on) is no longer as brutal as it once was and may not be necessary. If it is needed, you will still need to be aware of the root cause of your problem so that it doesn't return.

Other vocal problems

It may be that your posture needs correcting – perhaps the root cause is poor alignment. Your speaking patterns may be placing undue strain on your larynx. This may be responsible for vocal hoarseness. You need to ensure that the good habits that are being given to you in lessons are not being undone by poor practice techniques.

Nerves

Many people suffer from nerves (not to be confused with excitement before a performance, or dread when realising that you are under-prepared). For some, there are distinct chemical changes in the body that seriously inhibit performance. You may wish to consult a doctor who may offer some options. Deep breathing exercises may be useful and you can sometimes distract yourself from your nerves by 'getting into character'. If it is not appropriate for the character to be nervous, then maybe you won't be.

Before performing, try the following:

- Lift your shoulders up to your ears very slowly and let them go. Imagine two weights in your hands, let your shoulders drop even lower then release.
- Imagine you have a tennis ball under each armpit and hang your arms over the balls. Swing your torso from side to side.
- Put your hands on the back of your ribs. Exhale completely and take in a long slow breath, feeling your ribcage expand underneath your hands. Try not to lift your ribs in front. Exhale slowly and repeat.
- Close your eyes and stand still and comfortable. Imagine you are giving the greatest performance of your life. Imagine the applause at the end of your solo. Then open your eyes, look straight ahead and imagine projecting your performance to the back of the hall.

2 Off you go!

In this section of the book, we will concentrate on:

• Learning and memorising your music.
• Try-out performances.
• Practice techniques and tips.
• The basics of musical style.
• Evaluating your progress.
• First performances.

♪ Learning to read music is not as difficult as it might seem! Think of it as a map: learn to read one and you will not get lost. It is worth the effort – you will not have to be reliant on other musicians and your improved self-sufficiency will help you be better prepared, and therefore more confident, throughout your musical life.

Learning your music

You have been given a piece of music by your singing teacher and asked to learn it. Where do you begin? First you must:

• Understand the basic structure of the song – how fast it goes and where the beats are (**tempo** and **pulse**).
• Read through and understand the text of the song.

Then you must go on to more detail and learn:

• The correct notes and rhythms of the vocal line.
• How the vocal line fits in with the accompaniment – where the gaps or rests are.
• How the accompaniment goes.

If you read music, then this is no problem for you. If you do not have this grounding, then you will have to find a more accomplished musician – usually a pianist – to help you sort out these basics. Make sure you learn the song *correctly* from the start. It is very hard to eradicate errors once they have become ingrained.

The basic structure

First check the tempo marking. The tempo can be either marked generally (for example, *adagio* or *allegro*) or with a precise metronome mark (for example, ♩ = 120). Next work out the number of beats in the bar – this will help you to understand and feel where the strong beats are in the music.

• In $\frac{4}{4}$, the strongest beat is the first, the second strongest is the third and beats two and four are weaker.
• $\frac{3}{4}$ usually has a strong first beat followed by two weaker beats.
• $\frac{6}{8}$ usually has two strong beats on one and four, with a lilting quality.

Once you have worked this out, there is no harm in marking the beats into the music but do make sure they are in the right place!

You should also:

• Make sure that you understand the 'feeling' of the starting key, so that you can register the feeling on any *change* of key.
• Make sure you understand any repeat or **da capo** signs.
• Be aware of pauses, slow-downs and speed-ups and indications of expression.

The text

Work on the text is vital – remember that this was the original inspiration for the composer. Try the following:

- Memorise the text at the outset of your learning. This will make everything else follow more easily.
- Write out the text in a notebook. If it is in a foreign language, then leave a line in between the lines of the text in order to write in an exact translation – that is to say, one that is word for word and not merely approximate.
- Read the text aloud. Where do the stresses fall? How do the stresses and the punctuation affect the meaning? Make sure that you really understand the text. Often the poetry of the lines makes exact comprehension difficult. Do not assume it does not matter if you don't know what you are singing about – IT DOES!
- Look at any repetitions of the text. Why do you say things more than once? Can you colour the words differently? This doesn't just mean putting the accent on a different syllable or word!
- Paraphrase the text and put it in your own words.
- Declaim the text in an exaggerated manner. Your muscles can learn the feeling of the sounds of the vowels and consonants.
- Try a 'speed run'. Speak the text, as fast as you can utter it, not worrying about comprehensibility. If you have a block about the learning of a specific piece of text, go from the end of the phrase before you forgot the words into the beginning of the next phrase. Exaggerate the tongue, mouth and lip movements. If you repeat this enough times, you will find a physical memory for this passage. Alternatively, work again through the meaning of the text to make sure you understand it in the context in which it occurs. How does the bit you forget link to the bit that you can always remember? Can you think of a word that will help you link the one passage to the other?

It is especially important if you are singing a song in translation to notice that the phrases may be different from the original language. Translators cannot translate exactly because word order and the number of syllables will be different.

Example

'Who is Sylvia?' by William Shakespeare (from *The Two Gentlemen of Verona*). Set by Schubert, Finzi and numerous others!

The text:

> *Who is Sylvia?*
> *What is she, that all our swains commend her?*
> *Holy, fair, and wise is she;*
> *The heaven such grace did lend her, that she might admired be.*
>
> *Is she kind, as she is fair?*
> *For beauty lives with kindness.*
> *Love doth to her eyes repair, to help him of his blindness;*
> *And, being helped, inhabits there.*
>
> *Then to Sylvia let us sing,*
> *That Sylvia is excelling;*
> *She excels each mortal thing upon the dull earth dwelling:*
> *To her let us garlands bring.*

Text analysis

This particular text starts with questions and answers. Verse one: 'Who is Sylvia?' – what kind of person is it that can attract so much admiration? Answer – she is holy, fair and wise; furthermore, she has been put here on earth, blessed by heaven, for the sole purpose of being admired.

In verse two, the questioning gets a bit more demanding. Perhaps the questioner is doubtful, or wants more proof. The question goes, 'well, that's all very well but can you prove that this girl is kind, because her beauty's not worth much without kindness'. And the answer from the admirer comes back straight away that 'yes, she is good; even the God of Love (known to be blind and so immune to beauty perceived through sight) finds comfort with her'.

So in verse three, having asked some questions and found some answers, the questioner is satisfied and announces that since Sylvia is worthy of acclaim, she should be celebrated! You can either imagine this as a dialogue between two people, or perhaps as an inner dialogue – the same person putting both questions and answers.

Breaking the text into smaller chunks, you can do some more detailed work:

- If you were reading the text aloud, where would you put the breaks or rests to make the sense clear?
- Would you perhaps separate holy, fair and wise? These are three quite different ideas.
- Does the sound of your voice change in any way – in speaking – to distinguish between the questions and the answers?
- Which word in each phrase is the most important? Can you change the meaning by changing the stress? For example, if you stressed '**all** our swains' you would mean 'every man' but stressing 'all our **swains**' might imply that 'all the men but not necessarily the women commend this paragon'! Play with these stresses and see how they change the meaning.
- Try to paraphrase the text, verse by verse, using as few of the original words as possible. This might come out something like:

  All the men in our village like this girl Sylvia. What kind of a girl can she be?

  Well, she's pure, pretty and bright; she seems designed by God to be appreciated.

  Ah, but is she also a good person? You can't be truly beautiful unless you are warm-hearted and considerate. Well, yes because Cupid (the personification of love) seeks to live in her eyes, seeing the world as she sees it.

  Well in that case, we must all sing her praises and tell the world that she is exceptional. No other woman – not even a human being of either gender – can match up to her. So, we shall festoon her with flowers.

After that, reduce the text to as short as possible:

  *Sylvia is said to be great. We examine the facts and find she is beautiful **and** good. Hoorah for her!*

Try this exercise with another song and see if you can give it a similar treatment.

Now for the music!

The notes

There are two ways of learning the notes. The first, for a singer who doesn't read music, is known as learning 'by ear'. Many exceptional musicians – mostly in musical styles other than classical – have come from this tradition. Essentially, the notes are played or sung by someone other than the singer and the singer imitates the sounds that they have heard. The other way is by recognising different intervals in the scale, which can be numbered one to eight. Each number in the scale has a 'feel' and you will come to recognise how the notes relate to each other.

Another important element is the ability to recognise how a note relates to the keynote. The leading note (for instance, B in a C major scale), will feel that it is leading up to the *tonic* – the main note of the scale (i.e. C, in this case).

In order to improve your pitching skills, find a well-known tune. Work out the intervals and then those tunes will continue to act as an aide-memoire. Here are some suggestions:

- A sixth: *My Bonnie Lies Over the Ocean* (**My – Bon**)
- A descending second: *Yesterday* (**Yes – ter**)
- A fourth: *Away in a manger* (**A – way**)
- An octave followed by a seventh: *Balihai* (**Ba** – octave, **li – hai** seventh away from the original 'ba')
- An octave: *Somewhere over the rainbow* (**Some – where**)
- Sixth – tonic, fifth – tonic: 'Music of the night' from *The Phantom of the Opera* (**Soft – ly, gent – ly**)

Choose some of your own!

It is also essential to know how the note in your melodic line fits into the harmony that the accompanist will be playing. It is important that you learn your music vertically as well as horizontally (musically speaking, that is!).

The rhythms

You can approach the rhythm learning in either of the two ways above (by ear or by understanding the musical notation). Once you have learned the correct rhythms you can try:

- *Tapping out the rhythm.*
- *Tapping the* **pulse** *of the song with one hand (or clicking fingers, or tapping with your foot) and speaking the rhythms of the song at the same time.*
- *Reading the text at a normal speed and then in the rhythm of the music.*
- *Stamping on the first beat of every bar while you are singing.*
- *Clicking your fingers or clapping on each of the rests.*

Make the music something that happens in your *whole* body, rather than just in your head.

The rests

Once you have learned each phrase in turn, you must make sure that you have also learned how the gaps between the phrases are arranged. How many beats 'off' do you have? Have you time to take a breath? Will you come off a note early in order to facilitate your breathing? Also, remember that the rests are not merely moments of repose where you have a chance to get your breath back and renew your assault on the melody! They are still a part of your emotional and dramatic journey and should be used expressively.

The accompaniment

If you do not play the piano, you will have to engage a pianist for this. You may find at first that even though you may know your vocal line very well, it may be unsettling when you first sing it with a pianist.

- First, allow the accompanist to play the piano part by itself. Does the accompaniment change your idea of the song at all? How does it illuminate the text?
- Now, hear it again – this time, imagine your own tune superimposed on to the piano part.
- Now play and sing together – be particularly aware of the piano part in your rests. This will help you fit the next phrase in correctly. Most errors in music occur because you don't really know how the music goes when you are not singing!
- Try to make the same inflections in the music that you made when you were speaking the text alone. This may mean that you are stressing a word (or syllable) on a 'weak' beat. How does this feel?

Learning from recordings or CDs

Recording yourself

You will have to have the agreement of your teachers but try and get into the habit of recording some of your sessions with your coach, teacher or accompanist. When you listen back, you must be very objective. You will only learn through experience what you should be listening to and for but you may well be able to hear something on a recording that you are not aware of when you are actually singing. This can be an aid to your sessions with your teacher; however, you shouldn't use the recording as a substitute for concentrating and learning in your lesson. If you think to yourself, 'it doesn't matter that I didn't understand that bit, it's on my mini-disc' then you will be bereft if the disc doesn't record, or there is some other malfunction.

Other people's recordings

Listening to these might seem like a great shortcut to learning your music and it is certainly a useful tool. However, if you rely on it as your only learning tool, be aware of the following:

- There may be mistakes or wrong notes on the recording.
- The interpretation may not suit you – for example, the singer may make a very long and flashy pause on a note, which may not be so flashy when you attempt it!

- The speeds chosen may not suit you – remember, your voice is your voice alone.
- The interpretation may be very idiosyncratic – if you sing the song as it is on the recording you will be signposting the fact that you have imitated it.
- You do not know how this singer arrived at the decisions they made. They may themselves choose to sing the song quite differently next time!

You must learn to tread a fine line between knowing what is accepted practice and what is your original idea. As a general rule, first learn the notes on the printed page before making decisions to change them. If you do listen to recordings, then listen to more than one singer's interpretation of the same piece.

Memorising your music

The sooner you can 'lift' the details of the music off the page into your consciousness and voice, the sooner you can make it your own. Get away from the printed page as soon as you can – it is often used as a crutch. Singers perform with their whole body and face. If you are glued to the music for too long, you may be putting into your physical memory a certain way of standing and performing that you will find very difficult to shake off. Trust that you have a photographic memory. Look at the phrase and then look away – you will often find that you can still see it in your mind's eye. From the outset, perform a phrase at a time, first with and then without the music in front of you. Allow yourself to make mistakes that you then correct.

Remember that it is not merely the structure of the music of the printed page that you are learning. The vocal mechanism is complex and needs time to absorb information *physically*. Mistakes in muscle memory are very hard to eradicate. Don't try to take on too much information at a time. Your memory – whether mental or physical – must not go into meltdown!

Until you have some experience it will be very hard to estimate how long it will take you to learn and memorise your music. Some people are simply quicker at memorising words and music than others; however, everybody can develop these skills. Do not wait until circumstances are perfect to begin learning music. You may use excuses like 'there is no available rehearsal space', 'I don't feel good' or 'I don't need to start yet'. Recognise these thoughts as the enemy! Most singers learn the hard way that music not learned in time and thoroughly enough leads to loss of self-confidence and an impairment in the quality of your performance. **Music will not learn itself!** You have only yourself to blame if you do not put in the required effort.

Try-out performances

Before you attempt a 'proper' performance, try singing the music in front of as many friends as possible. It may be that an audience of friends and peers is harder than an anonymous paying audience but persevere. It will certainly feel different from the rehearsal. Give yourself the same rules as for a 'real' performance:

- You must not stop.
- You will have to cover up any mistakes that you make.
- You must have poise but not so much of it that you leave your personality at

Stay calm at all times! The more methodical and unhurried your preparatory learning is, the more reliable the foundations are for your music making.

the door! Most audiences want to be entertained and to feel that the singer is *human* and not merely a technically perfect machine! Never forget that audiences rarely come to hear a performance of perfectly executed scales and arpeggios. You must communicate the song.

- The audience must feel that you are experiencing this song for the first time. Even though you have practised it for a long time, it must not feel as if you are on automatic pilot. You should endeavour to keep a feeling of spontaneity.
- Assuming that you have done methodical and thorough preparation, you will be able to allow your inspiration to take over. This means that you can live in the moment. It may make the performance completely different from the rehearsal but this can be a good thing, illuminating the song for you in a host of different ways. Don't feel you have to force things to be the same.

Post try-out performance assessment

You will find out whether your memory or your voice is adversely affected by the pressure of an audience during your informal concert. It may be that a song that is fine in rehearsal is not in performance. Was it your nerves? Or had you not prepared enough? Perhaps you find a different key might be better. More importantly – did the audience enjoy your performance, even if you thought it could be improved upon? Did you enjoy it? Discuss these points with your teacher so that improvements can be made.

The only way to get better at performance is to have experience of it. Find as many performance opportunities for yourself as you can.

Practise and be perfect

The most important thing to do after selecting a singing teacher is to work out how you are going to practise. Where and how often are you going to do it? How will you know *what* to do? You will work this out closely with your teacher at first but over the months and years you will come to have greater individual responsibility for devising an effective strategy for practice.

What is practice?

Usually done alone, practice is time when you explore your voice and repertoire. Initially, you will be looking at the fundamentals of singing – breathing, tone, freedom of sound, uniformity of sound across all registers, clarity of vowels, stretching your range, finding support and making the muscles of articulation (tongue and lips) effective. These will be explored with exercises devised by your teacher. They will probably be a mixture of old and new exercises.

As you progress to music rather than exercises, you will use your practice time to do several different things. You should experiment with different speeds, breath patterns and vocal colours. You may choose to concentrate on perfecting difficult technical passages. You should think about the words. You must memorise the words and music as soon as you are able.

Practice is a solitary activity, thus it is very difficult to master. It is very easy to devise all kinds of excuses to avoid it! It is also easy to practise the things that you can do, rather than those you can't do! You must be very self-motivated and disciplined.

Where does practice happen?

Practice can happen in any space but ideally in a spacious room. Each room in your house will have its own acoustic and you want to find a balance between the over-resonant bathroom and the very dry lounge where carpets and curtains soak up sound. You should feel uninhibited in this space and happy to experiment. Remember that practice facilitates performance but is not always entertaining to other people in its own right – you don't want to be worried that passing children or flatmates will overhear and mock you!

Do not use the lack of a *perfect* place as an excuse not to practise! Think imaginatively – is there a church hall you could use? Do you know friends who have a large room you could use? You must find a solution, as effective practice is the key to vocal development.

Warming up

In order to practise effectively, you must first warm up your voice. Your teacher will obviously give suggestions and warm-up exercises are manifold! They could involve any number of different things but will probably include:

- Something to encourage **good concentration** – *a yoga breathing exercise, for example.*
- Something to remind the student about **good physical alignment***. Look in a mirror and find a strong position for the spine with the crown of your head aligned with the base of the spine. Your neck is long and your chin neither juts forward nor presses back. Your weight is evenly distributed between both legs and you are not leaning forward or back from the waist. Your stomach muscles are strong and your chest is neither pulled too far up nor collapsed.*
- Something to **energise the whole body** *and get oxygen whizzing round your bloodstream! This will involve some of kind of exercise that will shake out the tensions in your limbs – shoulder circles, hand and wrist shakes, unlocking and flexing the knees, movements of the ribcage and so on.*
- A **breath exercise***. For example, make a long aspirated 'sss' sound, pulling in the lower abdominal muscles as you exhale. Hold on empty. When you take a breath the abdominal wall will drop down allowing your diaphragm to drop too. The in-breath will be taken as a kind of automatic reflex.*
- Something that **engages sound and support***. A 'brr' lip flutter or a rolled 'rrr' up and down scales gets the air going with vital muscles supporting the sound. Make sure you don't drive air to get sound out or to reach top notes. The air pressure should be easy and even throughout your range.*
- Something to keep the **throat open** *and the* **vocal folds together***. Gliding on an 'ng' sound throughout your range is a good start. Keep it smooth and quiet – there should be no bumps as you change registers. Don't force the sound at the top of your range and do not get louder as you get higher. If you find it hard to go seamlessly from one register to another, then slow up the slide until it is effortless. At all times, imagine that you have a big smile inside your throat, as if you could laugh at any minute and this will ensure that your throat is open.*

Each singer has to find their unique way of warming up and to discover it you need to become aware of how your body works.

Pick and choose between warm-ups. Invent some of your own!

Don't start a lengthy practice session without warming up your voice first, however, don't spend so much time on warm-up exercises that you never get to the practice proper! Once your voice is warmed up, you are now ready for …

Technical practice

Your teacher will give you appropriate exercises depending on the 'method' you are being taught by. The principle is that you will be made ready and able to sing anything that a composer asks of you. Exercises could be specifically aimed at muscles and may involve making 'noises' rather than 'singing'. It is likely that you will concentrate on one area of technical development at a time, only moving forward when you have reached an understanding of the technical area in question. Exercises could be aimed at enhancing your musicianship, involving work with the voice on different intervals (a tone, semitone, octave, etc.). They could be developing skill in flexibility – scales, parts of scales, arpeggios. You will probably prepare the same musical material on all of the different vowels, in order to develop evenness of tone. You will have a range of fast and slow exercises.

A little pause – rest and recovery

Now you will have been working for a good while; probably between twenty and forty minutes, depending on your level of expertise. It is time for a rest! You must build up stamina gradually. Take ten or fifteen minutes and make a cup of tea or have a glass of water. Don't use the rest time to make a phone call or chat to your friends – that is not voice rest.

Music practice

You have chosen your piece and learned the notes securely. What now? Are there any tricky passages that you have not mastered? Devise ways to rehearse them that are not merely singing the song from beginning to end. You must have a clear plan. The fundamentals of voice production must remain at all times – throat free, jaw relaxed, breath low, support working, tone matching (no forcing, gripping or shouting!).

Fast passages with lots of notes or runs

If the passage has complex runs in it, you will be able to relate these shapes to the shapes of some of your singing exercises. You can practise many different things to make them come more easily:

- Practise them under speed.
- Practise the 'basic tune' – usually the first of each group of notes.
- Break the runs down into turns and mordants, trying to articulate them clearly but in small sections or 'cells'.
- Practise them in different rhythms.

> **Example**

'Rejoice greatly' (from Handel's *Messiah*)

G. F. Handel

Original run (b. 20 onwards)

etc.

Basic tune

Run broken down into turns and mordents

Triplets

Quintuplets

Septuplets

Dotted rhythm

Dotted rhythm reversed

For difficult jumps you could try:

- *Sliding between the notes slowly.*
- *Singing the notes lightly and very short, jumping from one note to the next and repeating quickly.*

For passages of very quick words – 'patter' – try:

- *Making the sound of all the consonants, leaving out the vowels.*
- *Pronouncing the consonants with huge energy whilst leaving the jaw open and still.*
- *Finding all the 'tip of the tongue' consonants – t; l; r; d; th; and so on, making sure that the tip of the tongue is articulating them clearly.*

For problems with breath:

- *Try playing the phrase on the piano and blowing out your air gently (without singing) – like through a small tube – for the duration of the phrase. If you cannot play, then follow the vocal line with your eye and blow air as above for the duration of the phrase, which you are hearing in your head.*
- *Then sing the phrase, remembering what the feeling was like to keep a constant stream of air. Many long phrases present problems because the singer holds on to their breath, making them feel as if they have run out of breath!*

Summing up: a checklist

- Do you know the text of your song apart from the music, or do you need the music to prompt the text? If you know each independently of the other your knowledge of the basic material will be deeper and richer.
- Do you know what the text means? Could you paraphrase it in a sentence?
- If the piece is in a foreign language, do you know what every word means, or only the general gist, or the singing translation?
- Can you sing your song from memory?
- Will you recognise the accompaniment? Do you *know* the accompaniment? Have you counted out the beats between your phrases? Try learning it as well as 'your' music.
- Have you thought about the structure of the piece? Where are its highs and lows? Where is the climax? Are there many thought changes or only one thought ('I love you, I love you, I love you!' for instance)?
- What are you trying to convey? Why did you want to sing this song in the first place? What do you want the audience to get when they hear it – a sense of how good you are or how good the song is? Can you convey to them the emotions that you feel?

At the end of your exertions, always leave time for …

The cool down

At the end of your practice you should still be able to sing! Don't be over-enthusiastic, forget the time and over-sing. Get into the habit of singing some of your vocal exercises at the end of a session. You could try:

- Breathing exercises – the same ones that you did at the start, perhaps.

Practice is something to be enjoyed and savoured, not got through as quickly as possible! Always leave time for reflection and concentration.

- Making the sound of vocal 'fry' or 'creak' – a relaxed throat sound almost like a dull rattle: this helps to relax the vocal folds.
- Gliding on an 'ng' sound again.

Mary and Tony's handy tips for practice

- Stand a few feet away from a full-length mirror. Make sure you are looking at your eyes and not your mid-torso. Practise your exercises and music performing to this 'other self'.
- Vary your practice – try standing still, walking around, sitting. The aim is not to get too 'fixed'.
- Record *some* lessons, practice sessions and rehearsals. Listen back to your recording. It will help you hear whether you are doing the things that you think you are doing.
- Perform singing exercises with musical and communicative integrity. In other words, don't practise like an automaton.
- In your keenness to sing and enjoy the sensations that it provides, you may forget to prepare, both physically and mentally. Effective singing and practice has a lot to do with mental clarity and concentration, and you may have to acquire these skills. Remember that this concentration is still in operation when there are rests in the music – don't switch off when you are singing.
- Rather than getting bogged down in detail, try using a stopwatch and consciously scheduling your time precisely. For example, you could decide to warm up for fifteen minutes. Set the clock and do it for exactly that long. The same could follow for other parts of your practice, whether technical or preparatory.
- Practise your songs unaccompanied – give yourself the first note and see if you end up on the right one at the end!
- If you are singing and playing the piano at the same time, be very aware of your posture, as it will affect your singing. Sometimes you can develop a kink in the neck as a result of always standing in the same place to sing – in a chapel choir, for example, or when standing beside the piano in a lesson or coaching session.
- Music stands can become a shield behind which you hide and they also will affect your posture – don't overuse them. Practise holding your music whilst singing, as it is a skill you will have to have for oratorio performance. See how well you can maintain good posture whilst doing this.
- When performing in a small room, try to sing beyond the walls of the room. Either look out of a window (but don't be distracted by what you see there!) or imagine that you can see through the wall.
- Your shoes are very important. If they are too flat, they throw your weight backwards. If they are too high, they throw it forwards. Practise in all sorts of shoes to prepare you for what you might need in production. In the lead up to a performance of a recital or oratorio, practise in the clothes you are going to wear. This will alert you to tight cummerbunds, floating straps and descending décolletages!

How to improve your musical skills

Most of us are musical and all of us can develop skill. All musicians need to develop an ear that hears more acutely than is necessary in everyday life. Singers need to hear intricate differences of pitch and rhythm, and to be able to relate a melodic phrase to the harmony around it: however complex the harmony, singers have to be able to maintain their own melodic line.

Singers are often called upon to sing in languages or accents other than their own and must be able to pick up subtle nuances of sound so that they can be taken for a native speaker of that language or district.

The notation, which gives us the hard facts about how the music is to be sung, is only a starting point. Life needs to be breathed into it. Each interpretation should be different and yet be within the parameters of the composer's intention.

How to improve your 'hard' skills

In popular music we think nothing of tapping along to the beat but this is not 'good form' in classical music. This doesn't mean that you should have no contact with the rhythmic pulse and feel of the music!

- When you learn a piece, feel the strong beats – do the same with all music that you listen to, whatever the genre.
- Don't be afraid of counting out the beats in a song, or writing them in your copy.
- Can you feel the 'back-beat' or 'off-beat' in $\frac{4}{4}$? It's very strong in popular music!
- Can you tap the strong beat with your foot and clap or click your fingers on the off-beat?
- Can you feel the lilt of a $\frac{6}{8}$ or $\frac{9}{8}$ piece? Can you hear the small notes?

You will need to be able to 'tune in'. You will have to hear your melody in your head *before* you sing it. You will need to be able to hear it as you are singing it. You will need to hear it when the accompaniment is playing. You need to hear both through your ears and feel sensations in your voice *and* body.

It is extremely important to know how the intervals of a song relate to one another. Singers often neglect to think about what happens when they travel between the notes. You must remember that you must keep the vocal tract open at all times and not try to 'find' the notes by squeezing, pinching or gripping the throat, or by forcing your body into violent contortion! Try the following:

- Play a note on the piano that is within your range. Sing it. Play another one, randomly, while you are still singing the first. Then, travel to the second note by sliding to it. Then slide back to the first note.
- Create a random melody, by extending to more notes within your range. Slide all the time, with open throat.
- Play a chord of three or four notes. Sing the bottom one first. Then slide to all the others in turn, singing all the time, rather than stopping to listen. Keep your throat open as you 'travel'. Don't be too cautious or come 'off the voice'.

As you become more confident, you will be able to analyse and repeat the intervals you are singing – you will thus have a sensation that 'fits' with each interval.

You cannot be singing aloud in all your rehearsal time. As you acquire more stamina, you will be able to sing for longer times but it is a good idea to vary the type of practice you do, in order to keep yourself interested and to ensure that you remain creative and playful. There is lots of useful work you can do to increase your skills that involves active listening:

- Listen to all music avidly, in a mix of live and recorded experiences. Let it 'wash over' you. Be aware of your feelings and of what the music suggests to you. Articulate those feelings and do not be afraid of using highly charged emotional words.
- For curiosity's sake, listen to three or more recordings of the same piece and chart their similarities, as well as their differences.
- Listen to three different singers singing the same song. Are they singing it in the same key? Are they singing it at the same speed? Are there any differences in the way they pronounce the words? Can you hear some words better than others? Can you work out why? Do they have the same feel? If you like one interpretation better than the others, do you know why? Is it just because you prefer the sound one singer makes, or is there something about the way they sing the song that touches you more?
- Can you identify the differences between singers in different styles of music? Try not to think about the SOUND of the voices (although that is important), or even about whether you LIKE one singer more than another. Concentrate on the style issues. For example, in musical theatre, the vocal quality might be more like speech than singing; in a pop song you may hear short phrases, or a breathy quality to the sound and the singer may phrase 'behind' the beat, or 'come off the voice'.
- Imitate all voices you can – can you make their sounds with your voice. Lower-voiced men; experiment with your falsettos! Women; explore the lowest and highest sounds you can. **Obviously, stop if it hurts.** Don't force sound while you are experimenting and don't prolong your experiments if they feel uncomfortable. You are only having vocal 'playtime'.
- Imitate accents you hear on the radio or television. Can you mimic Australian? American? Cockney? (Depending on where you are from!)
- Copy sounds, rhythms and inflections that you hear around you in everyday life. Stimulate your ear!

Remember, if it hurts, don't do it!

You must become aurally hyper-aware. You will need this 'resource centre' of vocal qualities as you continue to explore a whole range of different music. Have fun! Be playful!

Mary and Tony's handy tips on the basics of musical style

Folksongs
Folksongs are amongst the first music of any culture. They can either be sung unaccompanied, or with a simple accompaniment. There are also 'art song'

versions with more complex accompaniments. Beginners are often asked to sing a folksong without accompaniment in order to learn how to hold pitch. You have to learn to hear the tune in your head where there is no accompaniment to support it.

Although the music can be repetitive, the phrasing is not. Each verse will have a different text and therefore emphasis will be given to different words within the phrase. Because of this, the tune feels slightly different each time. Many folksongs, though not all, tell a story. You are expected to make the text clear and the story comprehensible. One common folksong structure is that of the verse and refrain. The verse carries the running narrative and the refrain – which always has the same text – acts as a breather between the story sections. This builds tension, as the audience has to wait for the next instalment of the story. You should be able to change the way that you sing the refrain in order to point the story.

Arie antiche

Translated from Italian, arie antiche means 'old songs'. These are the collections of songs, generally from the seventeenth and eighteenth centuries, which have been employed over the ages in the teaching of singing. It is thought that Italian is the easiest language to sing in – it has the purest vowels and the least obtrusive consonants, and is therefore the language that most encourages a fluid line in singing. This can be linked to a style of singing known as 'bel canto'.

You might also be given Vaccaj exercises to learn, which are miniature versions of arie antiche. They build musical and vocal skills incrementally. You will learn them in Italian even if you are at an early stage in your singing. They are not as narrative in structure as folksongs but inhabit a world of strong emotion, and can be quite dramatic and declamatory.

English song

English song has had two flowerings. The first was in the sixteenth and seventeenth centuries, and includes music by Dowland, Campion and Purcell. The second was in the late nineteenth century and early twentieth century with a wide range of composers including Warlock, Quilter, Gurney, Elgar and Vaughan Williams.

Dowland and Campion are amongst a group of composers who wrote for lute and voice. Their songs are definitely art songs and, though they are quite small-scale (volume wise), they incorporate a large range of emotions. Purcell makes great demands on a singer. Whilst he did write some simple strophic songs, many of his best vocal pieces are mini-dramas. The singer needs all their creative and imaginative power to convey the music as it travels through myriad changes of mood, tempo and dynamic.

The later period of English song is, in general, very well crafted for the voice and includes many well-loved songs.

Singing in the language that the audience understands is something that every singer should be able to do. For example, singing a well-known English song to a British audience is a good way to get them on your side. You must, of course, be clear!

★ Birgit Nilsson, after singing a heavy batch of Wagner operas, would return to Sweden and 'restore' her voice by singing arie antiche.

📖 **Bel canto** (meaning 'beautiful singing') – a cantabile style of singing usually associated with the Italian school.

Recitative

Recitativo is an old Italian word, translated as recitative though it corresponds to our word 'recitation'. In music, it refers to the attempt to deliver text at a speed that corresponds to speech. Since the text has to be projected (into large halls for example) and has to match up to the sung arias, which it usually precedes, it is sung rather than spoken. This speech-like quality is known as *parlando*. The pitch is often quite restricted, almost like a priest intoning in a church. The rhythms tend to follow speech patterns and you should try to make the delivery as naturalistic as possible.

There are two kinds of recitative. Normal *parlando* recitative, known as *secco* or 'dry', is recitative accompanied by a keyboard and sometimes a bass instrument (for example, cello). When the recitative becomes more emotional, it becomes more sung and is consequently supported by an orchestra. This recitative is called *accompagnato*.

Composers have developed certain conventions in the way they write recitative down. In fact some of these notational devices are misleading. Performance practice has passed down a series of conventions about how you actually interpret them. These include:

- You should not necessarily sing in tempo.
- You can go through rests if it makes more sense of the text.
- You can shorten the long rests, unless there is some harmonic activity in the accompaniment.
- You can play with note values to help the stress of the words.
- You can add extra **appoggiaturas**, if you think it helps the text but don't let it hold up the speed of the delivery.
- You can also add rests for expressive effect, as long as it doesn't hold up the action.
- You must retain the ability to be flexible in delivery. Recitatives should sound as spontaneous as improvised speech.
- In general, you should be able to sing the recitative as quickly as you can whilst retaining the sense of the narrative and the clarity of the text.

Where the secco recitative has an accompaniment that is bound up with the singers' vocal line, *accompagnato* recitative is often like a dialogue between the orchestral accompaniment and the singer. Sometimes the orchestra will react to the singers' line; sometimes it will anticipate it. Emotions are heightened. Usually, it is a bridge between secco recitative and an upcoming aria or duet. The vocal line will be more sung and less *parlando* and in tone, it is almost the same as in the aria. The rhythms are flexible but the tone is full. You have to really know the orchestral part, as it will help you make many of your interpretational decisions. Spend time living with the recitatives – experimenting with ways to sing them pays dividends. They can even help you set up ensuing arias in a way which makes them much easier to sing.

It is quite likely that **secco** *recitative will give few technical problems. The secco recitative may not be the most interesting part of a role. There is not necessarily a tune you can hum! However, make sure you spend enough time on them and do not try to 'wing it' on the day of a performance. Sometimes even finding the right starting note can be a challenge.*

Appoggiatura – *a leaning note, a grace note, which carries the accent and takes a certain portion (usually half) of the value of the principal note following it. It is often created by a suspension.*

N.B. In music of the classical period (including Beethoven and Schubert), when an appoggiatura precedes two principal notes that are of the same pitch and duration, the appoggiatura replaces the first of these.

'Thy Hand, Belinda' (from Purcell's *Dido and Aeneas*)

Purcell

Musical analysis

- Learn the exact note values.
- Then, sing with a strong feeling of two in a bar, not four.
- Take each phrase in turn. Each phrase must stay in the same tempo for the duration of the phrase; however, the *next* phrase can be at a different tempo.
- Be aware of the dissonances – for example the A♭ in 'darkness' which clashes with the basic chord of C major.
- If the harmony changes significantly on a rest – as for example the rest before the text 'on thy bosom' – give the rest the full value in order to experience the chord change before singing the next phrase.
- Appoggiaturas can be added and should be selected according to the importance of the individual words. For example, 'invades me' can be F and E instead of E and E. Most of the others are written out by Purcell, for instance, 'bosom' and 'death is *now*'.

Dramatic scenario

Purcell made decisions for you by setting the text in a particular way. You the *singer* need to respect the notes. However, you the *character* only know what you are saying at the moment you are saying it; you the *character* do not know the phrase that you are about to say. You have to find a way of making the performance seem unpremeditated.

Despite the fact that Purcell has made many decisions, you still have to make your contribution. There is much drama contained in these eight bars – it is not merely the warm up for the lament that follows! You have to decide how you are going to present your version.

Firstly, are you sure you *understand the meaning*? There are seven separate phrases and some of them could be interpreted in more than one way:

Thy hand, Belinda = give me your hand (because I need your support).
Darkness shades me = my brain is beginning to cloud over *OR* I feel odd *OR* I am about to die.
On thy bosom = on your shoulders, chest, body.
Let me rest = let me lean (let me take physical comfort and strength from you) *OR* let me catch my breath.
More I would = I want to do more *OR* I want to say more *OR* I want to be showing courage.
But Death invades me = I am overcome by the nearness of death *OR* I am in too much pain to speak *OR* I have no time because I am so near death *OR* I am suddenly overcome with terror.
Death is now a welcome guest = I must accept death *OR* I want to die *OR* I am glad all my torment and anguish is over.

Imagine the *general* scenario:

- Have you *already* killed yourself – that is, taken poison, stabbed yourself, for example?
- Are you going to kill yourself *after* the lament that follows this recitative?
- Are you coming on to the stage weakly, or desperately?
- Are you calm or agitated?
- Do you feel frustration and anger at your inability to speak more, or are you resigned and relieved?

The important thing is to make a decision and try it out. If you don't think it works, try something else. Thinking about the above questions and supplying your answers will already take you part of the way to an individual performance.

The *rests* between phrases, and the tempo of these phrases, will vary according to how you intend to play out the scene. Notice how a different scenario changes the way you breathe – for example, an agitated anxious Dido will sound different from a resigned and relieved one. You want to *colour your voice* in as many appropriate ways as you can. What we do not want is generic emoting. In other words: do not sing a sad song, sadly! It may be that despite the minor feel of the whole recitative, you can find a glimmer of hope – perhaps the last line becomes energised and positive, rather than tragic. Do not confuse making expressive decisions with being overly physical. You do not need to throw yourself about the stage or act out the piece with lots of physical gestures.

Musical theatre style

The musical theatre singer aims for a *natural* vocal production – effortless and attractive. The musical theatre singer can have vibrato, but not too much, and they must be able to control it (and take it out when requested to!). What matters most is how they express the words, as they are often described as 'singing actors' – the conveying of text and the understanding of character and context are of crucial importance. They may be required to sing in a 'character' voice, with lots of bite or 'twang' on the sound, for example, Annie's 'I'm just a girl who cain't say no' from *Oklahoma*.

Speech singing

The techniques that a classical singer uses for recitative are very similar to the way that a musical theatre singer sings the 'verse' part of a verse-and-chorus song. When you sing the verse, you may have a lot of freedom with the tempo. There are likely to be short phrases. You must find a happy medium between speaking the lines and singing them – if in doubt, listen to see how Fred Astaire sings!

First, find out what pitch your own **speaking voice** is. Talk as you normally do and then try sustaining your speech on one note in the same register as your normal speech. Match this to a note on the piano. It is usually thought healthy to speak quite low – around A to E at the bottom of your voice, although of course there are exceptions. This is a very individual thing and you may need to learn to place your speaking voice in a new place.

Phrasing and the text

All notes are not necessarily of equal duration in a musical theatre song, even when they are notated as such. You always go with the natural speech inflection of the rhythms of the words. Begin, however, with learning the rhythms exactly as the composer has written them down. You can only be free when you have mastered the information that is on the page.

Long notes

There are choices to be made with long notes and not all of them are notated in the way that they would be in classical music. There are certain conventions:

- You might not sing the whole note length.
- You may start a note quite loudly, but then instantly get quieter or 'decay' so that the impact of the note is at its start.
- You may start a long note with no vibrato and then introduce it at the very end of the long note to 'warm' the sound.
- You may crescendo into the next note of the phrase.

Evaluating your work so far

How do you know how well your singing is going? Your teacher will be the first person to give you feedback but how do you learn to evaluate your own work? At the beginning of your study, you are constantly bombarded with information – you may find it hard to process it all.

Goal setting

Evaluation is easier if you first set tangible goals for yourself. These must be specific rather than general. For example, 'I am trying to be a successful professional' is a very long-term, general and ambitious goal. You should learn how to set more achievable goals.

- They could be technical in nature:
  I am thinking of keeping my throat open/... of how I am jumping that interval/... about making the text clear/... about keeping a settled speed without rushing and so on.
- Or they might be about performance and communication:
  I am looking at myself in the mirror and never dropping my gaze from the reflection of my own eyes/... I am singing beyond the walls of this room.
- Or about the dramatic context:
  *I am Susanna and in the aria that I am singing, I need to be sure **I** am thinking what **she** is thinking, at **the exact moment** she is thinking it.*

After you have sung, you will need to give yourself time to reflect on what you have done and how it felt.

- *Did you keep your throat open all the time?*
  If you did, then well done! If there was a place where you failed, then perhaps you need to do the exercise again or having isolated the part you find difficult, you may need to wait until you are with your teacher to get a better result.
- *Could you look at yourself in the mirror all the time?*
  If you couldn't, try again. Perhaps you are looking away when there is a technical problem, or when you don't know the words. You can analyse for yourself why this might be happening.
- *Were you staying in character?*
  You may observe that you were trying so hard to sing the top notes that you forgot everything else! Try to shed any technical concerns in your practice.

Sometimes, the singer is so worried about how their voice *sounds* that they cannot express themselves musically, or they cannot inhabit the feelings of the character they are portraying. Practice must sometimes involve work that is not technical, or the singer will become an automaton. Don't be in a rush to go on to the next thing. Reflection is a necessary part of evaluation. To focus your practice, and to make evaluation easier, make sure you only do one thing at a time.

Responding to challenges

Make sure you know why you are learning a piece. Your teacher may have selected a piece for 'experimental' purposes. For example, perhaps to give you a feeling of a more expansive phrase, you may be set some Puccini. You may love it, and love the feeling of singing it, but it does not mean that it is ready for public consumption! Always consult with your teacher before singing something publicly.

You may not like a piece of music you have been set. Try to work out why. Do you not understand the words or the composer's intentions? Have you heard a performance of the piece that you didn't like? Does the harmony put you off? Try not to reject things too quickly.

Do you worry about a note or passage that you cannot at the moment master? Sometimes your technique is not equal to your imagination. For example – for artistic reasons, you want to sing a phrase really quietly. You cannot actually do this with your throat open yet, because that is a technically very advanced thing to do. It may be that this is a piece you should not spend an enormous amount of time on but, instead, come back to it at a later stage of your technical development when it will be easier to achieve your aims.

First performances

At a certain point, you may decide to sing *for* people – possibly an informal gathering of family or friends. It is important to test yourself in front of an audience, so that you can discover whether nerves – which are inevitable – throw you off your set course or not. In performance mode, you should think of communicating your pieces to the audience. You should not be worrying about technical imperfections. Audiences will forgive many imperfections if you communicate well.

There are many distractions around you – a new space, a new acoustic and the faces of your friends, which weren't there when you were rehearsing. Do they put you off or do you enjoy the freshness this brings to the occasion? Is your pianist suddenly and unexpectedly nervous? Does something happen which has never happened before. If so, how do you deal with it, knowing that you cannot just stop and start again?

After the performance, you will receive many comments – positive, negative, incomprehensible, personal, helpful, not-so-helpful, and so on. You will only learn with experience how to deal with these and we will cover this in more detail in a later chapter. For the moment, try to keep your nerve and stick to the plans you have made with your teacher and your colleagues.

You won't always have an exact memory of how your performance went as you may have been carried away by the emotion of the text and music. Later – on the same night, or the next day – you should reflect on the whole event. Run through the programme in your mind and recollect what happened. Was the performance different from the one you had planned? Were there musical or textual mistakes? How did you cope with them? What did people say and do you agree? Is there any feedback that you wish to give further thought or discuss with your teacher? Is there something that you can just discard – this may be helpful information but not immediately useful to you. For example:

> **Audience member:** 'You didn't sing that song quietly enough'
> **You:** 'I know, I can't do it yet. I'm working on it.'

> **Audience member:** 'Did you know you lift your eyebrows every time you sing a high note?'
> **You:** 'Hmm, no, I must look at that … '

Sometimes, general comments are helpful because they point out things you were doing that you didn't know you were doing. However, resist the temptation to

In order to help remember your sequence of songs, find an imaginary journey from the beginning to the end of your programme. Instrumental soloists use this method for concerts and recitals to take over as a safe aide-mémoire. It does not matter how crazy a journey it becomes!

list all the things you did 'wrong'. Don't preface your reflections with 'I didn't do 'x' every time. **Make a list of everything you did 'right' first** – 'I got to the end of the recital without going wrong or tiring', 'people really enjoyed it', 'I felt brave and not uncertain', 'I stayed with the pianist on the difficult transition', 'the pianist said I sang well', 'I remembered the words', and so on. You must learn to be positive. It is not about being boastful but about making honest assessments and keeping a balance between skills achieved and skills yet to learn.

3 Halfway round the course!

In this section of the book, we will concentrate on:
- Singing coaches.
- Language coaches.
- Some examples of singing in different languages.

Introduction to advanced section

At this point in your studies, your teacher will have guided you through various exercises to an understanding of your own voice and your strengths and weaknesses. They will also, by and large, have chosen your repertoire for you. You will have delved into music by many different composers and discovered what your preferences are. As you improve, you will notice that your teacher makes more demands upon you. You will now have to perfect things that for a time you could let go. Each level of improvement comes at a higher cost. To be good is hard; to be very good is much more than just doubly hard!

At this stage, it may be that you are harbouring ambitions to be a professional singer; you may be excited at the prospect of earning your living by music. You will therefore need to raise your game and make greater demands upon yourself. If you are to become professional, and in order to raise your standards even at amateur level, you will need to:

- Know how to practise *effectively* and have some sense of how to evaluate your progress.
- Have reliable vocal stamina.
- Be less dependent on your teacher for repertoire.
- Be less dependent on your teacher for every interpretative suggestion.
- Be able to research effectively, finding out the context of your pieces.
- Be able to translate languages, or able to organise help if required.
- Be able to assess how much rehearsal you will need and also be able to organise it, by communicating directly with other musicians.
- Be open to new ideas and also have definite ideas of your own that you can defend articulately.

There is a fine balance to be had between practice that makes you stale and no practice at all. Some singers delude themselves into thinking that not practising a piece too much will create a fresh and spontaneous performance. This is a very risky game. The best way to perform with enjoyment and pleasure – and therefore to give the audience the same experience – is to be confident in the music and your mastery of it. This may mean that you will allow more time for practice, since you will hopefully have acquired some stamina. After a while – and exactly how long will depend very much on individual circumstances – you will become more self-reliant.

However, you must not forget that with this ever-increasing demand for greater skill, you must endeavour to maintain your love for singing. If you can retain the joy that you felt when you first began to sing, there is a good chance that your audience will feel it too.

Singing coaches

Why do you need them?

- You mostly hear your own voice through your facial bones and not so much through your ears.
- If your voice is well projected, then less voice is heard within yourself.
- The acoustic of a room or hall will reflect your voice and often give a false impression of it.
- You need to become familiar with the accompaniment that the coach plays for you.
- You need to know if your voice is communicating what you intend it to.

What do they do?

They can give you objective feedback on your singing. They can help in the following ways:

- Helping you to learn the notes.
- Assisting you to memorise.
- Helping you to understand the style of music.
- Helping you understand the dramatic context.
- Giving you vocal hints, by reinforcing your teacher's work.

♪ *The coach is there to ensure that you are as well prepared as possible for rehearsals and performance.*

Learning the notes

Coaches can help speed up the learning of the music. Knowing the role or piece of music well, they can impart information about the shape and structure of the music. They can help you unravel any strange notation or stylistic quirks – this is particularly helpful in working on contemporary music.

They can double your vocal line whilst playing the basic harmony underneath. This develops your confidence and ensures that you are singing the right notes and rhythms. Coaches take on the responsibility of correcting any mistakes, so that you can concentrate on the singing and the physical sensations of it. When correcting mistakes, the singer needs not to worry about 'being wrong' but concentrate on the different sensation of the *right* note. A coach allows you to repeat until you are really certain of the corrected passage. Repetition is vital because you need to be really confident about singing with an accompaniment.

Your coach will know the *orchestral* sound (when applicable) as opposed to the piano reduction. They will be able to play the piano in such a way that you are prepared for the completely different feeling when you sing with the orchestra. This will save time in expensive orchestral rehearsals. There may be things that you cannot hear as well in the orchestra as you can in the piano. The coach will illuminate these for you, which will enable you to be better prepared. Some accompaniments are more supportive than others. Here are some characteristics of a few of the difficult ones:

- **Continuous** – the sound never stops and there is no waiting for you (for example, in Bach). You need to find a way of breathing without holding up the flow.
- **Loud** – that is, an accompaniment with which you seem to be at war! It is hard to 'be heard'.

- **Beautiful** – the audience's ear is continually drawn to it and away from your singing. You have to 'earn' the right to be heard.

Coaches can help you project your voice over the accompaniment by:

- Making sure that the vocal entries are clearly defined.
- Helping you to decide where to breathe.
- Helping you decide when it is acceptable for you to shorten the note values in order to facilitate breathing.
- Helping you sing right through the phrase *beyond* the last note.
- Encouraging you to discover new 'vocal colours' for each phrase, that are suggested by the text.

 In order to find new colours in your voice, imagine a slide show with a picture for every single phrase and change the slide between every phrase. React to each image to 'colour' the next phrase.

Assisting you to memorise

It is important to test your memory in front of someone else. This person can help you by:

- Improving your strategy of memorising: for example, repetition of short sections, pointing out memory 'traps' – the places where it is possible to take a wrong turning.
- Pointing out inaccuracies in the music and text so that you improve with each repetition.
- Formulating strategies to help link specific words and sections together, sometimes using mnemonics and alliteration.
- Prompting the text just before you sing each phrase in order to encourage you to look away from the page of music.
- Singing the other parts in pieces for multiple singers, which is a real help to memory. When you are practising alone, you do not hear those bits and they will either put you off or, make your life easier!
- Guiding you in your choice of passages to practise in future. A coach is always alert to the weaker memory moments: a coach sometimes hears a hesitation before you do!

Understanding the style of the music

Sometimes you need guidance when venturing into a new style of music and a coach can:

- Explain the background to a style and give you some idea of the composer's possible intentions.
- Explain the notational differences between differing styles: for instance – a '>' over a note can mean different things according to the composer in question. It could mean that you accent the note, or you might have to lengthen the vowel, or you have to lean on the note. An understanding and knowledge of pieces by the same composer will enable the coach to determine which it should be.

Understanding the dramatic context

The coach will know the whole piece (opera, oratorio, song-cycle, and so on) from which you might be singing only an extract. They will therefore be able to:

- Illuminate the context in which the number occurs, which will help you to …
- Explore the dramatic journey of the character or poet.

They will also be able to assist you to translate the text and explain its meaning.

Vocal hints

A coach can add to what your singing teacher tells you by:

- Understanding your singing teacher's individual technical language and act as a 'third ear' in order that you can find out how the voice sounds.
- Ensuring that consonants are clearly enunciated.
- Ensuring that vowels are given full value and are differentiated clearly.
- Checking your intonation, particularly as it relates to the harmonies in the accompaniment.
- Helping you choose and compose embellishments where appropriate.

This last point needs a little embellishment itself!

Embellishment, ornamentation and runs

These are all used in most periods of music. They are almost always a way of heightening expression. Assume that there is a basic tune or melody. The composer, or the convention like the **Da Capo aria** (which your coach will guide you in), will invite you to 'add' some extra notes. This might be at a cadence point, or it might be within a phrase.

Embellishment is normally a small event: a flourish. It can fill out an interval between two notes. For instance, there is an octave between two notes of our basic melody. It can be filled out in several ways, by different patterns – a diatonic or chromatic scale, an arpeggio or even a series of turns. Something as simple as an **appoggiatura** (a leaning note) or an **acciaccatura** is an embellishment. As will be evident from your vocal exercises, scales, arpeggios and turns are the basic shapes found in all music. Your regular exercises should give you a good vocabulary of possible embellishments.

In seventeenth- and eighteenth-century music, **runs** were one of the ways that composers expressed emotion. They did not have to be fast – they could be lyrical and slow. The singer must learn them slowly, in order to maintain real line over all the notes. You must not put accents on the main beats to help you know where you are in the phrase. The **syllables** of the text should not interrupt the flow – the text is an unimportant vehicle for the notes. Of course, you must fit in all the syllables so that it makes sense!

Ornamentation is the practice of adding notes. In the eighteenth century, performers were expected to be able to improvise these at the moment of delivery. Nowadays, we usually work out in advance what we are going to sing. As a rule of thumb, do not go outside your own range and try to stay within the compass of the aria, even if you happen to have many notes outside it. Try to find more imaginative ways to 'fill in' intervals than a series of scales! **DO ask the coach for help.** Remember to fix ornaments in advance, so that you have enough time to practise them – it is often like learning a whole new piece.

 **Da capo aria** – a baroque aria, which is in tertiary ABA form and where it is normal to ornament the repeat of the A section.

Acciaccatura – short grace note before a principal note, to be sounded as quickly as possible. Marked with a line through the tail of a quaver.

 **Coloratura** – 'colouring', ornamental passages runs, trills, and so on.

The coach will help you to understand the sensation of shaping runs. It should rarely feel like a ricochet of notes: the runs should be clearly articulated, without overdriving breath. There should be no intrusive 'h's. The coach has a great role to play in helping shape the contours of the runs imaginatively. They will guide and confirm that the runs sound clean and clear. A coach will also let you repeat and adjust ornaments until they are best suited to your voice.

Be warned that ornamentation is a contentious topic! You may have fixed ideas and the conductor may have *other* ideas. You may have to change. Also, be aware that there are stylistic differences between different composers and this will be reflected in your choice of ornamentation – what is right for Handel is not right for Bellini.

Language coaches

One of the differences between operatic or classical singing and musical theatre is that classical singers have to be prepared to sing their music in the original language. Furthermore, it is becoming the norm that you will be required to sing in languages other than the standard Italian, German and French. These might include Spanish, Russian, Czech and even Hungarian, Polish and Swedish.

Before you can work with a language coach, you will first have to be responsible for doing some groundwork. If you are working on a language new to you, you will have to do preparatory work with a language specialist. They may put the sounds on tape, or they may give you a transliteration to help you master new sounds and alphabets. The groundwork includes being sure of the correct sounds and being able to translate the text *word for word*. It is not enough to have a general sense of the text's meaning. In order to know which are the expressive or important words in a phrase, you will have to understand the literal translation rather than a singing one or a paraphrase.

You should be attempting to give the impression that you are a native speaker of whatever language you are singing. It is important that you sing more than a series of unconnected sounds, however correct they may be. There is a good chance that your singing will be beautiful if your language is exquisitely declaimed, fluent and resonant!

Why can language coaches help you?

- They will ensure that your text is beautifully **enunciated** and correct.
- They will be able to enlighten you about the language and its **meaning and context**.
- They will give you insights from a **native speaker's perspective.**
- They will ensure that you have an appropriate **balance** between the music and the language.

The best language coaches are the ones who understand music and singing. You may be tempted to think that a speaker of a language, who is not a musician per se, will be able to instruct you sufficiently. However, it is the case that there are conventions in the *singing* as opposed to *speaking* of most languages, which only specialists understand. Remember that you must know your music well, as you will have to sing for the language coach as well as speak.

Working on your own

Once you have worked with the language coach in some detail, you will be expected to work on your music by yourself in a constructive way. Try the following approach:

- *Try singing the music on the vowels alone. Let the vowels flow into each other.*
- *Now 'touch' in the consonants gently. Try to imagine them on the actual note. The vocal line should be interrupted only minimally.*

How do I adjust the text to the speed of the music?

You may have learned to speak a language correctly but find that when you sing it to certain music (slow tempi, long phrases, declamatory passages) you have problems. Try:

- *Reading out the text of your piece out aloud in its own natural rhythm at a conversational speed.*
- *Read it slower and then slower still.*
- *Read it in the tempo of the music and without 'marking' the beats i.e. let the natural flow and intonation of the words be retained.*

Now:

- *Sing the text on a comfortable note in your range, maintaining the correct inflections of the text whilst singing. Ensure that the inflections of the text do not interrupt the flow of the delivery of the note. Make sure that you do not 'bump' significant syllables.*
- *Sing the 'right' melodic line. Do not let it affect the natural intonation of the words or their meaning. If the tempo is slow, then the vowels will have to be 'stretched'. Please do not stretch the consonants!*

With all of the above in place, you must achieve a natural delivery. Your singing must not sound like a recording slowed down! Never get sloppy with articulation of the consonants.

How do I make sure that I am true to the composer's intentions?

Singers, anxious to keep faith with the composer and their intentions, are sometimes worried that work on the text without the music may contradict the wishes of the composer. However, the importance of your individual work on the text cannot be underestimated. You must know the text thoroughly in order to understand where the composer is 'coming from'. Remember that the composer started with the text and that is where you should begin. After you have explored the text, you will see how the composer has chosen to emphasise certain words. The musical techniques used to create emphasis include the following:

- A **long note**, which creates a long vowel.
- **Delaying** an important word or syllable, by use of a rest before the chosen word or by rhythmic means such as syncopation.
- Making a word expressive by indicating an **appoggiatura** or an **ornament**.

The first language: Italian

Almost all singers begin with Italian because it is reckoned to be the language of singing; even a beginner student in classical singing is expected to tackle it at an early stage. Good Italian enunciation involves the following principles:

- Italian vowels are rounded and never distorted. They are often described as pure.
- There is a continuous flow from vowel to vowel, whatever the intervening consonants.
- Single Italian consonants, which are more 'liquid' than in English, do not interrupt the vowel flow.
- Double consonants create a characteristic hiatus in the flowing line, which can be very expressive.

The language coach will help you to elide vowels in the text correctly. Sometimes there are many vowels clustered together on one note and it is important to know how to place them. Remember that:

- Vowels flow from one to another with no intrusive sounds such as a 'y'.
- Your tongue, and not your jaw, manoeuvres the vowels.
- The muscles of articulation (principally, the tongue and lips) make the consonants.
- Any consonant that can be hummed ('m'; 'v'; 'n') should be!

A language coach will also show you:

- That consonants need to be on the note to which they are attached and not on the preceding one.
- How not to overdo 'plosive' consonants, such as 'b', 't' and 'p'.
- That a single 'r' in the middle of a word and between two vowels, is always flipped and not rolled.
- That the rolled 'r' is for beginnings and ends of words, and when it is attached to another consonant.
- That two vowels together generally have equal value.

A good coach will also help you with **portamenti**. The difference between this and what is called a 'slide' or even a 'swoop' or 'scoop' is that a portamento ensures that:

- Both notes are in the same vocal position – you don't change registers on the way.
- The 'carrying over' is done on the first vowel. The vowel only changes when you have reached the next note.

All the arie antiche (literally 'old songs') of the seventeenth and eighteenth century provide good practice for singing in Italian.

> **Portamento –**
> *a particularly expressive feature of Italian singing, literally meaning 'carrying over'. The note is joined to the next note by a connection or glide.*

> **Glissando –**
> *a slide in the voice between two notes.*

Example

'Lascia ch'io pianga' (from Handel's *Rinaldo*)

Try 'Lascia ch'io pianga' from Handel's *Rinaldo*. It looks simple but needs detailed attention to all these aspects of the language.

Lascia	Allow (from 'lasciare', imperative form)
ch'io	that I (shortened from 'che io'. The use of 'io' creates emphasis to 'I')
pianga	would cry (from 'piangere', subjunctive form)

la dura sorte	the hard fate ('r's between vowels are only flipped, the 'r' in 'sorte' is rolled as next to another consonant, also rolled at the beginning and end of words)
e che sospiri	and that would sigh (from 'sospirare', subjunctive form)
la libertà	the freedom (accent marked on last syllable, where generally, in Italian, it is on penultimate syllable)

Try saying the text at the tempo of the song. See how slowly it goes!

Other languages

Having a good understanding of the Italian language will provide a firm basis and secure technique for singing in other languages. We are now going to consider, in brief, some of the principles of singing in French, German and English.

French

French is a complicated language relying on clearly enunciated vowels. As in Italian, there is very little vowel modification. 'Mouth shapes' are very important. The three possible shapes are:

- Smiling – as in 'chat'.
- Lip kissing or pouting – as in 'doux'.
- Gormless, with dropped jaw and loose forward tongue – as in 'âme'.

French vowels

There are many more than in Italian. In addition to the Italian vowels, there are five other pure vowels and four nasal ones. Despite their name, nasal vowels should not to be completely 'put into the nose', as this would prevent the sound resonating in the mouth. A language coach will help you find a satisfactory placement for them.

Mute endings

The singing style of the French language demands that the vowel at the end of a word which is normally silent in spoken French, is sounded in order to aid the audience's comprehension of the word. For example, 'presence' is sung as three syllables as opposed to two. The mute ending will need to be 'lifted' and placed in a 'forward' position whilst still sounding like a weak syllable. It should not collapse at the end of a phrase. It should be used to place the exact ending of the word.

Consonants

Be careful not to over elongate consonants. You should not anticipate them before the beat, unless it is for an expressive purpose. Such anticipations will only be used in very special moments.

Elision

This is where the end consonant of one word which is silent when spoken, is sounded at the beginning of the next word. The rules governing this are complex and subjective. Your language coach will be able to help you to decide what is appropriate.

Emphasis

The most natural way to emphasise a word in the French language is achieved by lengthening the vowel. Many composers, such as Debussy and Massenet use a line above the note to indicate this.

In French there are no sudden accents as in German and English – fluidity is the primary goal!

Example

Clair de lune by Paul Verlaine, set by Debussy and Fauré

Let us take an example from the French Mélodie *Clair de lune*.

> *Votre âme est un paysage choisi*
> *Que vont charmant masques et bergamasques*
> *Jouant du luth, et dansant, et quasi*
> *Tristes sous leurs déguisements fantasques.*

First we need to decide on where the elisions should occur – normally they will occur everywhere except where there is a comma or there is no connection of sense. So we can elide the first four words so that each syllable ends with a vowel:

Vo – tr'a – m'e – t'un

We do not elide 'luth' and 'et', or 'dansant' and 'et', because of the commas. These decisions on where to elide will need guidance from your French coach.

Watch that the nasal sounds as in '**vont**', 'char**mant**' and 'dan**sant**' have no trace of the 'n', since this is only there to indicate a nasality. Note that though 'déguise**ments**' ends in a nasal sound, when the '*ent*' comes in the third person plural of a verb it is a mute sound: as in 'they sing' – 'ils chant**ent**'.

In Fauré's setting, you have the problem of creating the effect of a mute ending on a long note – as in 'bergamasques' and 'fantasques'. Feel the syllable lighten and lift away.

Watch the difference between the open and closed 'e' – open as in 'est' and closed as in 'et'.

Words such as 'charmant' and 'dansant' need to be expressed by energising the first syllables, even if they are set off the main beat.

Remember – French is a fluid language and has no invasive accents.

German

German will feel stronger and more resonant than French.

Vowels

Although they are basically the same as in English, there are two new concepts to grasp. There is an extra sign to learn – the two dots above certain vowels. Known as **umlauts**, these indicate a different shape for the vowel in question. They can be over an 'a', 'o' or 'u' vowel. You must take care not to make the sound too shallow or pinched. Your German coach will teach you how. The second new feature is the 'schwa' or neutral vowel. For example, the last syllable of 'vergess**en**' must sound like a weak syllable but must not be dropped. Like the French mute ending, it has to be placed correctly. Additionally, your coach will prepare you for using long and short vowels appropriately.

Vowel onsets

German, like English, has a characteristic gap before words that begin with a vowel. Usually, it needs only a small hiatus to separate the two sounds. When it is an important word, then you can use a glottal stop or shock for stronger emphasis. It is important to learn how to make these sounds without causing undue vocal pressure.

Diphthongs

These are double vowels crushed together as in 'We**ei**nen'. The stress is usually on the first of these two sounds, the second sound should be delayed as long as possible. It is important to make the 'glide' between vowels sound effortless and clear. Make sure that your tongue – not your jaw – is doing the movement from vowel to vowel!

The 'ch' sound

A written 'ch' will be affected by the vowel that precedes it. When it follows an 'a' vowel it is lightly gutteral and must not disturb your vocal quality too much. After 'o' and 'e' it will be less guttural and it will be at its softest after an 'i' vowel. The soft one as in the German word 'ich', mustn't sound like an 'sh' (English '*sh*oe') but neither should it be too hard (English 'si*ck*'). Try to pronounce it like the name '*H*ugh'.

Example

Schubert's *Lachen und Weinen*

Let us take the first line of a Schubert Lied:
Lachen und Weinen zu jeglicher Stunde (Laughter and weeping at any hour).

If we sing this on vowels alone, keeping as close to Italian vowels and omitting dipthongs, we get:

'A – er – u – ai – er – u – e – i – er – u – er'

Notice that the 'schwa' vowel 'er' needs to be given equal resonance with the normal vowels. Be aware of the long and short vowels – long as in the first syllable of 'Weinen' and short as in the first syllable of 'Stunde'.

To give the consonant sounds their English equivalents, the consonants 'nd' at the end of a word become 'nt', the 'w' is pronounced as 'v', the 'z' is like 'ts', 'gl' becomes 'kl' and the 'st' at the beginning of a word becomes 'sht'. The consonants can be joined together as follows:

'l – ch – n / ntv – n – nts – y – kl – ch – sts – nd'

Notice the separation (represented by /) before 'und'. There are lots of consonants that can be 'sung', like the 'l' of 'lachen' and the 'v' at the beginning of the word 'Weinen'. Even though we need *all* of the consonants, don't forget to spin the sound on the vowels!

English

If this is your mother tongue, you will think that you know it already, however, there are pitfalls in singing in your native tongue. You may need to make yourself *more* aware, as accents and dialects that you may have in speech may not be appropriate in your singing. Be sure to examine the text without the music so that you are really certain what it means. Look carefully at punctuation marks, which have a significant bearing on meanings! The English language has certain inherent difficulties:

- It is not such a resonant language as, for instance, German. We are more softly spoken; therefore English needs more work to help it to 'sing'.
- We have quite a lot of 'dull' or impure vowels and many diphthongs to negotiate.

- We are often lazy in pronouncing consonants properly and run them together imprecisely.
- Final syllables, such as in the last syllable of the word 'forgotten', are often swallowed.

Furthermore, in a language which you speak and which you have no conscious memory of learning, you may be careless about some of the language's potential for precise expression – some words are very subtly different!

Vowels

The rule with diphthongs is the same as it is in German – the first vowel has the bulk of the time. You will need to be aware of whether the pure vowels are long or short. For example, the word 'feel' has a long vowel sound. If you shorten this sound unintentionally, you may actually pronounce the word 'fill' which clearly has a very different meaning!

Glottal onsets

As in German, where there is a word beginning with a vowel, make sure that you separate the sounds efficiently and without too much of an attack, unless it is an important word. This is a significant element in making your text clear.

Consonants

The final consonants of words and phrases are vital for comprehension. For example, you sing a word that begins with the syllable 'be' but you fail to articulate the final consonant. What does the audience imagine it was? Was it: 'beak', 'beam', 'beat', 'beast', 'bean', 'bead', 'beef', or 'beep'…?

Even if you don't have an English coach per se, make sure you have feedback from your singing teacher and your coach. It is also useful to have feedback from audience members – as your teachers will work with you over a long period of time they may stop correcting you!

Example

'How beautiful are the feet' from Handel's *Messiah*

Let us take an example from Handel's *Messiah*.

How beautiful are the feet of them that preach the gospel of peace'

First, practise this on vowels alone, as underlined above. Notice the distinction between long and short vowels. For instance, the words 'preach', 'peace' and 'feet' have long vowels. 'Gospel' and 'of' have short vowels. Now take the consonants out of the sentence and find how they can be 'crushed' together in 'clusters':

H – b – t – f – l / r – th – f – t / f – th – m / th – tpr – chth – g – sp – l / fp – s

If you cluster the consonants together you can save a lot of effort and loss of air by singing them as one sound instead of two or three separate ones. Notice that the meaning of the sentence demands that there should be a feeling of a comma between the words 'them' and 'that'. There are also slight separations, marked above with '/', between the words 'beautiful' and 'are', 'feet' and 'of', and 'gospel' and 'of'. You could choose, however, to elide some of these.

Final consonants are important, such as the '*t*' of 'feet' and the '*s*' at the end of 'peace' but there is no need to spit them out. Find a way to spin them within the line of the sentence. Always adhere to the shape and stresses of the language.

♪ There are no absolute rules with musical theatre but a myriad of choices – the overwhelming need is to put the text and its meaning first.

Singing English, American and other accents in musical theatre style

Diction in musical theatre is extremely important. Text, and an understanding of it, always dominates over vocal line – you must make yourself understood. You may be required to adopt an accent and this will be determined by the dramatic context of the piece in question. For example, Eliza Doolittle in *My Fair Lady* sings in Cockney and then later, after her transformation, in R. P. (R. P. stands for **Received Pronunciation** – upper-class English, if you like!). In a full production, the director will normally decide on the approach to accents within the cast and there will be dialect coaches to assist if the accent is very specialised. However, there are some conventions – *Les Misérables*, originally in French, is not sung in a French accent when performed in English.

Most singers are expected to be able to sing in a convincing American accent, as America is the 'home' of the musical. Be aware in particular of the need to pronounce the 'r' sound within a word or at the end of a word. It is a common misconception that Americans pronounce 't's as 'd's, or leave them out altogether!

When singing in musical theatre style, you should always place the punctuation marks, having slight pauses for commas, for example. However, placing a comma is not the same as taking a breath or taking time – you must learn to place the tiny gap without disturbing the pulse of the music. You are aiming for a delivery that sounds as close to a natural speech inflection as possible.

Words beginning with a vowel should be placed with space before them, although the strength of the glottal shock or stop will be down to individual judgement.

If singing songs from a musical with a 'pop-like' feel (*Mamma Mia*, *Rent* or *Grease*, perhaps), then the delivery of the consonants may be more like that of a pop song, when they are slightly slurred. Try not to over-pronounce consonants – 'r's should not be rolled and consonants should be articulated clearly but efficiently. Where there are two consonants together, you don't necessarily need to pronounce both and certainly not with a vowel between them!

Example

'Send in the clowns' by Stephen Sondheim (from *A little night music*)

Words and Music by Stephen Sondheim

First of all, speak the lines naturally without any reference to how they are notated. Then, try and speak them in rhythm without being too rigid in the quaver movements – they are not all quite equal (as they are notated) but slightly different as they would be in speech (think of how a Dalek would speak the words – this is NOT the effect you are after!). Do not, however, get too free with the how the tune appears within the bar – you must still try and get all the notes into the time available – don't 'back phrase' as your only method of expression. Back phrasing is the habit of stretching so that it takes longer than the bar but where the rest of the accompaniment goes on without stretching. This means that you are singing your melody notes to the 'wrong' harmony. It differs from rubato, which is an elasticity of tempo where all performers agree to do the same amount of stretching or 'pulling around'.

When you begin to sing the lines, keep as close to the spoken quality of sound as you can. With long phrases, put all the commas in – you don't have to take a breath but it would be good to have a space:

- *One who keeps tearing around / one who can't move* – but later
- *Losing my timing this late in my career* – should be sung without a break as it makes better sense of the line.

When there is a word starting with a vowel in the middle of a phrase, you have the option to put a small space before it, or elide the last consonant into it, or put a hard attack on it (the glottal stop) – this will be dictated by taste (either yours or your musical directors'), or the sense of the text. You can also have this break before a word that you want to emphasise but which starts with a consonant. For example:

- I*sn't – it rich* – slurring the 't' gently into the 'i' but in the next line
- *Are we / a pair* – putting a break between 'we' and 'a' because that emphasises the text better.

The phrase 'one who keeps tearing around' doesn't need too many breaks in it, as it lessens the point of the 'tearing around' – so you should elide these words into each other. It may be that you choose to urge the tempo forward here and then pull it back for 'one who can't move' – this also describes musically what you are saying in the text.

You definitely need a gap between:

- *My fault / I fear* – but so small that it doesn't use up much time! And then later:
- *// I thought that you'd want what // I want* – glottal attack for emphasis and
- *There // ought to be clowns* – glottal attack for emphasis

The whole first verse could go as follows (but you may decide to make different choices!):

Isn't – it rich

Are we / a pair

Me here / at last / on the ground; you – in mid – air

Send – in / the clowns.

// Isn't it bliss?

Don't you / approve?

One – who – keeps – tearing – around / one who can't move

Where – are the clowns?

Send – in the clowns.

Singing in translation

You will often find that you are required to sing in a language that is not the original one. The ultimate goal is to make the translation sound as natural as the original. The rhythms of each language are distinctive, thus the original rhythms of the music may need to be slightly adjusted in order to make the translation sound colloquial and smooth. You should always attempt to sing the translation as written. As you gain more experience and status, you may well be confident enough to alter translations to suit you better (and even to improve on them) but do give the translation a good chance before altering it. If you know the piece in the original language, it may take time to adjust to the new words.

Whatever language and style of music you are singing in, you must convey the text clearly, unaffectedly and correctly. If you are singing in a language that is not native to you, your aim is to be understood by a native. Sometimes you can *speak* a language well, and understand all the grammar, but be incomprehensible when you *sing* in the langauge. The expert help you have at hand with language coaches can really make a difference to your communicative confidence! Remember that the text contributes at least 50% of your performance as a singer and that beautiful language produces exquisite singing.

4 The going gets tough – being tested

In this section of the book, we will concentrate on:
- Auditions.
- Exams, competitions and awards.
- CVs and biographies.
- Being business-like.

Introduction to classical audition section

Everybody knows auditions are not the ideal way to judge vocal and dramatic talent. However, the fact is that they exist and until somebody finds a better way, you will have to learn audition skills.

You should assume that the audition panel is on your side and wants you to be good. They want to find budding talent. They want to find the right person for a role or a concert and you must learn to help them choose you! Here are some of the most commonly asked questions about general auditions:

Who do I audition for and how do I apply for one?

Your teacher and coach will advise you as to an appropriate starting level. The most frequent error is that singers try to audition at too high a level, too soon. Auditioning is a skill, for which you need to build up confidence gradually. Don't be unrealistic or too ambitious. To apply, you will usually write to the auditions secretary and ask when the next general audition will be taking place. You may have to send in a CV in order to be invited to audition.

Can I avoid auditions by inviting the panel to come and see my performances?

Yes but be aware that bombarding casting departments with invites won't necessarily make you popular! Usually, agents and casting directors have a good idea of what performances are happening around the country. In addition, several people will need to hear you: music staff, director, conductor, administrator. As it is unlikely that they will all be able to get to your performance, auditions are a way of them sharing the same experience of your singing. Of course, reputation can and does spread by word of mouth. One of the panel may have already heard a performance of yours, without you knowing.

Why do they hear me in a small room and not on a stage?

Small companies often don't have a permanent theatre and large companies will not have very much available stage time. Experienced panels can tell how your voice will project in a larger space.

How will they know how 'big' my voice is?

Experienced panels can tell in a moment what your vocal qualities are. Curiously, it is always possible to imagine a voice *bigger* from hearing *lighter* repertoire than the other way around. A common mistake that singers make is to sing repertoire that is too big for them.

Will they be able to judge my potential?

It is vital that you sing what you can really sing *now*. Let the panel have the excitement of imagining where you might go from here. Don't try to demonstrate your vocal potential and the things you can *nearly* do! What is important is that the panel want to be able to cast you *now*: they need to see something usable. If you sing repertoire that is thrilling in parts but seriously flawed in other places it will do you no favours.

What should I take to sing?

Take something that is completely within your grasp. Don't choose pieces that only work when you are feeling on top form. Choose pieces that show off your different talents: fast runs, high or low notes, slow long lines, skill with text, communication of character. Remember that what you omit from this list is significant. For example, if you are a tenor and you sing pieces that have no real top notes, the panel will assume you don't have them. If you are a soprano and you choose a specialist high piece, such as the Queen of the Night from Mozart's *The Magic Flute*, make sure that you can really sing it! In other words, don't do what you can't do just because you think the panel expect you to. Sing repertoire which helps them reach a definite decision about **what you do best.**

How many pieces should I present?

A good auditionee will have a stock of five or six arias, from which they can select three to take to a first audition. They should be of varying periods, languages and styles – not all fast or slow, or all by the same composer. There is no reason to avoid the standard repertoire; in fact it can help the panel. If you choose an unusual piece, the panel may be more fascinated by the piece than by you. For this reason, if you do want to offer something unusual then make sure that one of your other pieces is a standard. Ideally, none of the audition pieces should exceed five minutes. Try to have a combination of short and long pieces, or have in mind some optional cuts.

Do I need to bring the music?

In a classical audition, it is expected. Make sure, however, it is not in loose sheets or encased in a shiny document sleeve. Loose sheets have a habit of falling off the piano (distracting!) and shiny folders might reflect light, which can make the music illegible.

Will they provide a pianist?

Usually, though not always. You will always be informed of what to expect. Even if they do provide a pianist, you can choose to bring your own. If you bring your own pianist, make sure they are well prepared.

Will I be able to rehearse with the official pianist?

Sometimes but not always. Even if you do, there will be little time, so make sure you are well prepared and have heard the piano part before. Make sure your music is legible and very well marked-up: starting point, repeats, cadenzas, ornamentation, rubato, where the piece ends. Be prepared for a shortened introduction and shortened transitions between verses.

What should I start with?

The panel will normally allow you to choose the first piece and after that will select from your other offers. You need to choose something that will settle your nerves, allow you to adjust to the acoustic and will immediately spark the panel's interest.

What should I wear?

Something comfortable, which makes you feel at your best. Be aware that you may well be walking with your back to the panel and so what you look like from behind is also important. There are different audition dress codes in different countries, which can be varying degrees of formality but generally, try to find a mid-line between glamour and comfort.

What if I'm nervous?

You probably will be. Try to think of nerves as 90% excitement and 10% fear – there is much more excitement than fear! Make sure before the audition that you have drunk some water so that you don't have too dry a mouth. Breathe deeply. Try to get into character. Try to think of how much you enjoy the music and how you would perform to an audience. Imagine the panel is that audience. Usually, mistakes that are the result of nerves are easily distinguishable from mistakes owing to poor preparation.

What is the best audition approach?

Obviously the goal of an audition is to get the job! However, if that is your *only* marker of how to measure how you have done in an audition, you are set for a life of disappointment. You may do a very good audition and still not get the job. There are many reasons for this. It may be because the part that you would be right for is already cast. Or, you have the wrong look and the director doesn't want to compromise his or her ideas. Your voice, although excellent, will not match the rest of the cast, or be appropriate for the venue. Think of your audition as you would a performance and enjoy it. If you arrange to do something agreeable after an audition – meet friends, go to a movie or exhibition, for example – it will help you put the audition into perspective.

Mary and Tony's handy tips for auditions

- Get into the habit of **arriving in good time** and so having enough time to compose yourself.
- **Arrive warmed-up**, in case there is no official warm-up space.
- You will have to deal with the fact that **auditions are not an exact science**. They are likely to involve you either hanging around for ages, or being asked to sing before your allotted time. You can do very little about the former. With the latter issue, you should not feel pressurised to sing before you are ready to.
- You must **develop a thick skin about overhearing other people's auditions**, especially when they sing the same aria as you have chosen.
- If at all possible, leave your outer coat and heavy bags outside the room with the audition secretary, so that you can **arrive in the audition uncluttered**.
- Bring with you **a curriculum vitae** that is on one page and a current photograph, even if you think your agent has already sent one[2].
- Remember that **you are being judged** from the moment you walk in. Auditions are often very short but within that time, every piece of information about you is being gathered and filed away by the attentive

Be polite to the audition's secretary in charge – that person may very well mention to the panel any examples of rudeness or temperament that they encounter. Be polite to the pianist for the same reasons!

2 For more information on CVs, see page 67.

panel. Some panels prefer you to go straight to the performing area without many formalities; others will shake hands. Take your lead from them. Don't be afraid of eye contact when you first speak with the panel, however, don't eyeball them during your performance. You will be told where to stand. Make sure you are not too far from the pianist, so that they have contact with you. Beware of advancing towards the panel, mid-stream and invading their space.

- **Announce your pieces.** Announcing your pieces has a double purpose – it lets the panel know what you are about to sing; it also gives them information about your speaking voice. Don't apologise for what you have brought, particularly if you know the panel have heard your chosen piece sung by someone else before you – each performance will be judged individually. You should announce your pieces concisely, without any discursive plot explanations – assume that the panel know the repertoire. At home, practise announcing the titles out loud. Make sure you can pronounce them accurately and clearly, particularly when in a foreign language. Do not attempt to get away with avoiding the title (by saying, for example, 'Dorabella's aria' – as there are two, you will still have to say which one!). You don't want the panel to be whispering to each other whilst you are singing.

- **Do not spend long talking to the pianist.** This is the case even if you meet the pianist for the first time in the audition itself. Assume that whatever you do, they will be able to follow your singing. If they begin at the wrong speed, come in confidently at the right tempo without grimacing or coming out of character. You must be responsible for establishing the right tempo for you.

- Generally, when you start to sing, **focus 'beyond the heads' of the panel** but still in their direction. Whilst direct gazing feels too confrontational and makes the panel feel uncomfortable, you should also be aware that directing your performance to the sides of the room will make you look unfocussed.

- In a general audition, **you will be presenting a scaled-down version** of what you might present on stage. You need to convey that you are comfortable physically without either standing stock-still or wandering about. The key is to have stillness with focus and if you want to move, move with purpose and not all the time. The same goes for gestures – if you make one, follow it through but be wary of making gestures whenever you come to particularly expressive moments or high notes. On no account should you bring and use props at a first audition.

- **If you go wrong, try to continue.** The panel will learn something about you from how you recover from the error. If things break down, ask if you can begin the section again. The panel will understand, however, do not restart more than once or they will suspect that you are ill prepared, rather than nervous.

- **The panel may stop you mid-stream** – do not be offended. Time may be short, or you might have brought a long aria. They may have liked you and heard enough, or may want to hear your voice in a different sort of music.

- **Do not be put off by the panel writing or talking amongst themselves.** Although this can be annoying for you, they MUST do this if they are going to remember you accurately. Between pieces, or at the end of your second piece, the panel may do some conferring. This will mean that you have to wait – try and stay calm! The pianist can be a good ally and you can always chat a little with them.

- **The panel may want to ask you some questions**, perhaps about what you have been doing recently. It may be that they are trying to clarify information on your CV.
- When the audition is over, **leave the room with confidence** and without a sense of disdain or shame.
- **Thank the pianist.**
- **Remember your music.**

It is a sad fact that many companies do not have the time to acknowledge your audition, let alone give you precise feedback. This can often make the singer feel very powerless. In general, if the company wants you, they will contact you and you will know when they do that your audition was 'successful'. However, companies and audition panels frequently have long memories and it may be that the seeds of an audition do not bear fruit for a number of months, or even years. It is all the more important, therefore, that you try to see your audition as a performance in itself.

Different kinds of auditions for classical singers

Music colleges

Whether you are auditioning for undergraduate or postgraduate study, the admissions department will inform you of what you should bring to sing. This will include a variety of types of music – for example, pieces from opera, oratorio and song repertoire. You will at some time have to sing recitative. You will have to show that you can sing in English and at least one other language.

You will be sent forms to fill in. Make sure they are filled out accurately and comprehensively. You will have to provide **references** from respected musicians and teachers – don't leave it to the last moment to ask them to provide one! On your form you will be required to write a **personal statement**. Try and keep the language simple, clear and un-emotive. Try speaking it out aloud and make sure it sounds like you! You will often be questioned about it.

As well as your prepared pieces you will have to do a quick study. You will be given a short piece of music approximately ten to thirty minutes before you are required to sing it. This is to ascertain how you deal with notated music. It is only part of the assessment and you should not panic about it! You may have to present some prepared spoken text, or you may be given some text to read unseen. You will also be interviewed. Be prepared to talk about yourself and why you want to do the course. Be able to talk about how you are intending to finance the course.

Music courses (summer schools, for instance)

You may do these auditions 'live' or you may have to submit a recording. Make sure that any recording is well produced and not too long. Show a variety of styles and languages. If the course is very particular, you will be told what type of music to sing. Your audition may be videoed. You will not necessarily be able to get any feedback.

This section deals with the auditions that have very precise outcomes:
- *For music colleges.*
- *For music courses.*
- *Competitions and awards.*
- *For conductors.*
- *For directors.*
- *For agents.*
- *In foreign countries.*
- *Stage auditions.*
- *For specific roles.*

Exams, competitions and awards

Exams, usually graded for difficulty and possible for all ages and musical tastes, are a good way to measure your improving skill. They also give you a short-term goal and a focus. Your teachers will help you with the repertoire, which will be selected from a number of given choices. This repertoire is designed to show skill across a range of different styles and qualities of music. You will also have to do vocal exercises and some aural tests, where you might be asked to repeat a rhythm or a melodic line played on the piano. From grade five upwards you will also have to do some written theory exams. Enjoy these opportunities to perform!

At some stage of your singing life you will probably enter a competition. These might be local or regional for which you could win cups and certificates. At a later stage, you might have to sing in order to get money for study; further on still, competitions may bring significant prestige, prizes and professional engagements. Competitions allow you to enjoy and explore your communicative skills. They enable you to see and hear other singers, and to get feedback from the invigilator.

Young singers hoping to study for the profession, either privately or in an institution, will need to apply for **bursaries** and **scholarships**. You must always try to sing something well within your capacity and something else that will indicate your potential. There will always be strict guidelines given to you, which you should take great care to respect. National and international competitions cover every stage of a singer's vocal and dramatic development. Make sure you only enter the competitions that are appropriate for you – your teacher will advise you.

> Prepare each round of a competition like a recital – it should feel like a performance. Get the audience on your side and forget the panel!

Competitions will sometimes consist of a series of rounds. You may be selected first from your CV, references or submitted tape and not from singing 'live' at all. There will usually be very strict guidelines:

- You may have to supply a birth certificate to prove your age.
- You may have to select from a given list of repertoire.
- You may have to supply exact timings for each of your pieces. It is important that you don't do a 'guesstimate' but use a stopwatch.
- If you are asked for a fifteen-minute recital, you must allow for the gaps in between. If you sing for twenty minutes you may well be disqualified.
- You may not be able to do the same pieces in each of the rounds.
- If the final round is accompanied by an orchestra, you will be asked to supply details of the key and the edition, so that the correct orchestral parts can be ordered.

You must know and research repertoire well in advance. This means that you know the exact speed at which you intend to sing, so that your timing is accurate and is also decided on the basis of *your* performance and not somebody else's recording. You must not guess vital details at the last moment, when the form needs to be submitted. You will not be able to change the repertoire at the last minute.

The competition prize could be money or an engagement to sing. Be aware of the competition's purpose when you select your repertoire.

During the competition

When you are taking part in a competition there will be many singers around you. You may worry that they are better than you, or know that they have an impressive reputation. Try to develop the mental skills that will help you stick to your own 'game plan'. You may want to separate yourself in some way, either physically or mentally. Don't feel pressured to make conversation. If you know your music thoroughly, then you have nothing to fear. You can only do your best. You can only be *you*. The difference between a competition and any other audition is that it is based on *now*. It means that you are being judged against singers of different voice types as well as your own. The other contestants may also be at different stages in their careers but all will be competing on a level playing field.

If you are selected for the final orchestral round, your rehearsal with the orchestra may be brief. You must be extremely clear about your intentions and knowledgeable about the nature of the accompaniment.

The panel of experts and the audience may not have the same opinion. Even if you don't win, there is going to be someone in that audience who likes you and they may be in a position to offer you work. Enjoy your time on the platform!

Conductors

If you have the kind of voice that is suited to the concert and oratorio repertoire, then you may be able to sing for the conductors of choirs – either choral societies or church choirs – who hold regular auditions for potential soloists. You should write to them, enclosing your CV and say that you want to audition. You should ask the conductor if they need to hear anything specific.

> Think about what the conductor is asking you to do before you breathe for that relevant phrase. The breath will then 'create' the phrase with a new colour.

In opera, as an advanced singer, you may well be invited to sing for a conductor with a view to taking a specific role in a forthcoming production. Be ready for the possibility of a 'working session', where the conductor will see if you can be flexible in your interpretation. They might ask you to do a number of things differently – for example, phrasing, dynamics, rubati, tempi. This is not a criticism of the way you have prepared the piece but gives an indication to the conductor of how you will cope with rehearsals. It is important not to be too defensive and to try out all suggestions that are made to you.

Directors

Nowadays, it is very common that a director will want to meet you before agreeing to a casting. They will want to hear you sing and they also might want to talk to you about their plans for the role, see what you look like and get a sense of your personality. It is important for them to cast the whole piece appropriately – although you may be very good, you may not 'fit in' with the rest of the cast or the director's vision. There might be some kind of working session. This can sometimes be in a 'workshop' format, rather than a one-to-one session, where a range of skills including movement, improvisation and working collaboratively are assessed. Be prepared to try something really differently, even if it seems to go against the music or the text. There are many styles of directing and you should learn to be adaptable as possible.

Agents

Sometimes, agents will have heard you in performance and will be considering you for representation. If so, they will ask you to bring several pieces to sing and will then choose what they want to hear. You should take pieces that cover the whole range of what you can do, whether it is in the field of opera, oratorio, song, contemporary music, baroque music, or light music. You should also bring along any recordings that you have made – even demo CDs – as well as any reviews, wherever possible.

After you have sung, the agent might say that they feel they can't represent you *yet*. Their reservations may have to do with whether they think you are *currently* employable. It may be that they already have someone on their books of the same type as you and they won't be able to get work for both of you. It may be, however, that they will follow your developing career with interest. Although they are not *officially* representing you, they will sometimes be prepared to offer you support and advice.

It is possible to contact agents directly, instead of waiting for them to contact you but you must have a professional engagement they can come and hear.

Foreign countries

An agent may propose that you sing for foreign opera houses or other musical representatives. You may want to try and audition independently for an agent in another country. You may not get work in a specific country unless you have representation there. If you apply to a specific foreign opera house, then you need to find out the name of the auditions secretary. It is vital that you sing at least one aria in the language of the relevant country and you should be able to speak, even if only a little, in that language.

Because Germany has so many opera houses, the system there is different. The normal method is that you first audition for a German agency. Different agencies are responsible for different geographic areas. They will know where the casting vacancies are and can often send you to an opera house that needs your type of voice. Thus, you need to be flexible about how long you can stay in the country. Be prepared for the competition to be fierce and for the time you are allotted for singing to be quite short. You may have to wait around for a long time because of the number of singers being heard. If you are sent on to audition at a particular opera house, the German agent will have advised you on what you should take to sing. The panel will probably want to test your sound in the acoustic and also to test your stamina, so there may be a lot of waiting around and you may sing a considerable amount of music.

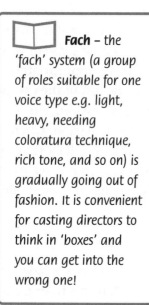

Although things have recently begun to change in Germany, be aware of the **fach** system where voices are grouped into 'compartments'. Each compartment consists of a number of roles considered to be applicable to one voice type, for example – soubrette, dramatic soprano, heldentenor, and so on. It is useful to be aware of what your fach is. It certainly used to be the case that you would never be employed to sing from more than one fach at any one period of time in your vocal development. Of course, as your voice changes, you might well move from one fach to another.

Stage auditions

If an opera company is interested in using you, after having heard you in a general audition or performance perhaps, you may be given a stage audition. This gives them a chance to hear you in the right acoustic.

- You will probably be asked to bring specific repertoire. Stage time is very restricted. You must be clear as to what the company wants to hear. If you are not certain what to sing, it is entirely permissible to ring up for some further clarification.

- You may be asked to sing a section of a specific role that is either an ensemble or a duet but without the other parts. This is because the hardest part of a role is often not the aria.
- The pressure of time can make you feel rushed and you may feel that your performance is suffering. **Forewarned is forearmed** – make sure you can go from one piece to another quickly, efficiently and without losing your dramatic and vocal commitment.
- When you announce your repertoire or speak to the panel, be certain to enunciate clearly and project your voice.
- The piano may often be far away in the wings or the orchestral pit and you may not be able to hear it very clearly. Trust that the pianist will be able to hear you and stick to your performance plan.
- Light may be poor so you must take time to find it. Feel it on your eyelashes. If you find yourself standing on a set from a current production, don't let it put you off!
- It is possible for you to move but don't wander aimlessly. Don't be tempted to enact the role, or explain the story.

Specific roles

You may be called in to have a working session on a possible role. The house in question will usually appoint one of their senior music staff to assess you. They might want to work on the ensembles, duets or recitatives. The session, and there might even be more than one, could be several hours long, since another of its purposes will be to gauge your stamina.

The working session is also really useful for you in determining whether the role suits you. Perhaps the *aria* is ideal but the *whole role* is currently too demanding. It will never be to your advantage to expose yourself before you are ready to sing a role. It is better to find out in a working session that it is too much, than to have pressure on you during production rehearsals, which might even force you to cancel.

In order to take advantage of the audition experience at whatever level, and not dread it, you must do as many appropriate auditions as you can. If you get used to this kind of performance – and it will always be best if you can think of auditions as performances rather than trials – you will discover which repertoire shows you off best.

Different kinds of auditions for musical theatre singers

The general guidelines for classical auditions apply to musical theatre ones as well. Specifically, what you sing will depend largely on your performing and casting strengths – that is to say, you will either be a:

Singer	actor	dancer
Actor	dancer	singer
Dancer	actor	singer

Obviously, all the permutations of these three skills are not listed above. 'Triple threats' – people who have equal skill in each of the three areas – are very rare.

☆ One example of unnecessary enactment in a stage audition is the case of a soprano who sang Barberina's aria from Mozart's 'Le Nozze di Figaro'. Though the experienced panel knew that at this point in the plot Barberina is searching for the pin that she has dropped in the garden, the singer chose to 'illustrate' the plot by crawling over the unswept stage and sliding her hands over the floor creating great clouds of dust! The effect on the panel was total embarrassment that the stage was not spotlessly clean and that they might be responsible for any dangerous bugs she might pick up. Her singing was not remembered!

Your primary strength (as a singer, actor or dancer) will determine the kind of auditions you go up for and therefore the sorts of pieces that you will present.

College and drama school auditions

You will have very clear guidelines from whichever institution you apply to. Expect to bring, memorised, some or all of the following:

- Up to three songs of varying styles and speeds.
- Up to three speeches with one of them a classical piece.
- An unaccompanied piece such as a folksong.
- At least one dance piece if you are a dance specialist.

Each school has different processes for auditioning. Expect that some of the audition will involve group work for which you are not expected to prepare. Dress appropriately for movement, or take a change of clothes with you. As places are in high demand there may well be a system of rigorous recalls. The school has to be able to cast shows, so must have a balance of gender and type. The competition – particularly for girls – is fierce.

Casting auditions

Some casting auditions are open to all and some need the recommendation of an agent. Open auditions require you to turn up early and wait for a very long time (often in the cold!) until you are given a number. It is sometimes the case that if you don't get there early enough, you will be turned away. Sometimes you can go away after you have received your number, knowing what time you will have to come back to sing.

- It is usual for the panel on these occasions to hear a very short section of your piece. This may be only **12 or 16 bars, which you will need to choose**. You don't have to start at the beginning of the song. You have to show what you can do in a very short space of time. You must show as much variety of vocal quality as you possibly can. If your song has a notoriously difficult section, you will be expected to sing that as your brief excerpt.
- As with all auditions, choice of key is important. With a pop or rock song, you should choose the key which suits your voice. With the musical theatre genre in general, you should be aware of the 'show key' – the key in which the song occurs in the show. There are now some very good anthologies available where all the songs are published in their original keys. Be aware that the keys in vocal *selections* are often VERY different from the show key, which means that you will not show off the right quality of voice.
- You may find a song where the vocal line in the treble clef looks stratospherically high. Check with an expert to see if actually this should be sung at the octave below.
- Beware of very long songs and try to choose pieces that can survive a cut. A 'story song' may be good when sung complete but sound very odd when truncated. If you don't feel confident with deciding which part of the song to sing or which key to sing it in, get another experienced musical theatre musician to help you. If at all possible your excerpt should have musical and dramatic cohesion.
- It may be that a role has a very specific vocal requirement – for example, a very high belt – that you will need to demonstrate in your audition.
- Wear something striking – this can be an accessory – so that you can be

easily remembered. However, it must not be a distraction or it may spoil your performance.

- If you are auditioning for a new show, try to find out as much as you can about it. This will help you take along appropriate pieces. You might choose something where the text or character has something in common with the character in the new piece in order to show your dramatic credentials.

If you have representation, or if your 'look' is right, you may be asked to audition or 'read' for a specific part. It could be for a solo role, or it could be for ensemble. You could be in the ensemble and cover (**understudy**) a solo role. In big West End shows with long runs, there are usually two covers for every large role. The 'swing', who covers many roles in the show but may not have their own part, requires a specialised talent.

Open auditions rarely lead to immediate castings. Of course you will be disappointed if you do not get recalled, that is natural, but try to see these auditions as experiences in themselves. You may find that something bears fruit a long time after your audition – casting directors keep very good notes and have very long memories.

Auditions follow a quite complex system of rounds or recalls:

The first round audition
You will usually take along two or three pieces of your own choice. You may have been requested to bring particular types of piece – a 1960s pop song, a ballad, a jazz standard, for instance. You might have to read something or bring a prepared speech.

Make sure that the pieces you take have a variety of fast and slow singing. You should tailor the chosen pieces to the nature of the show you are auditioning for. However, if you are short of time, you should sing something that shows you at your best, even if that is not what the show itself requires. This is because if you sing well the panel may think of you for another show for which you are better suited, or want to hear you again with a different piece. By singing something that you barely know in order to fit a requirement you may not show yourself off well. If you are in any doubt, consult your teacher and coach.

If the piece in question is a 'dance' piece (for example, *Cats* or *Chicago*), then the first round will also include a dance audition since, however well you sing, if you cannot do the dancing you will be unusable in the show.

The recall
♪ Recalls in musical theatre can go on for weeks – try to be patient and look at each round like a fresh challenge.

If you have been successful at the first audition you will be asked to bring more specific material to a recall. It may be that you will be requested to bring something from the show itself and will have been provided with some music. At this stage the panel will talk to you to find out more about you and your singing and acting.

Further recalls
With commercial theatre there is big financial investment and the backers need to be sure that they have the best cast available. Recalling can go on for some time as you work in increasing detail with the musical director, director or choreographer. It may be that you sing to one group of people and then later for another, more 'prestigious' panel.

Choices of music

Musical theatre singers must be up to date. Depending on your voice quality, you will need your standard pieces from older musicals and a range of other material. Be wary of getting stuck in the 1980s! Try to find new pieces from the most recent shows, in preference to a lot of more hackneyed numbers. Panels will have heard the same songs countless times and an unusual piece can really help you to be memorable. You should have – according to suitability – songs in each of the following categories:

- A classic musical *e.g. Rodgers and Hart or Rodgers and Hammerstein.*
- A standard *e.g. Gershwin or Cole Porter.*
- A Broadway song *e.g. Kander and Ebb.*
- A modern musical theatre piece *e.g. Webber.*
- A contemporary piece – *this will always be changing but for example, Jason Robert Brown.*
- Pop songs of each decade – *some of which should be folk-pop and some rock-pop.*
- Something that shows your 'legit' voice – *this means your 'legitimate' or classical vocal sound, so you need a ballad that shows the quality without the free embellishment of a pop, jazz or soul number.*

Your portfolio of songs should cover a range of dramatic and musical material. You will need up-tempo and ballad; you should have a narrative song that tells a story, as well as emotional ballads. If you are a character type then you will need humorous material. If it is appropriate, have some operetta, Kurt Weill, Jacques Brel, and so on – these are slightly more specialised areas. Always be on the lookout for new material to enlarge your portfolio, in order to be ready for every casting requirement.

NB for Classical singers

It is true that some shows require classical singing skills and classically trained singers often want to explore musical theatre as an area of potential employment. Be aware though that you must show that you have a good knowledge of the very different style of musical theatre singing. This is particularly true for girls. You should be aware of the following:

- Controlled/ absent vibrato.
- Different phrasing styles.
- Belting.
- Surrendering the vocal line to the expressive demands of the text.

A beautiful sound will not be enough! If you are serious about wanting to make a career change into this area, you may be best advised to seek further training.

CVs, biographies and photographs

CVs

The first thing to remember is that written information should be as concise and clear as possible. Try to put it on **ONE PAGE OF A4**! If you have a lot of experience, remember that you don't have to put down everything you have ever done.

You will almost certainly have more than one version of your CV or biography. Which one you use will depend on whom you are sending it to. Experiment with fonts and layouts until you have something you are pleased with. You want it to be clear and interesting but not look too fussy. It is useful to have a small photograph in the upper right hand corner.

SECTION 1: Background
This should take up no more than a third of your page and should include the following information:

(For classical singers:)
Name • **Voice type** • **Date and place of birth** • **Visa details** (if applicable) • **Contact details** • **Agent's details** (if applicable)

(For musical theatre singers:)
All of the above but add **range** (your highest and lowest notes) and the styles of singing you specialise in, for example – **pop, rock, gospel**. It is also common to add specific information about your **belt range**, for instance – **strong, high belt to F** (if true!)

- **Education** – starting with the highest qualification and working backwards. You don't need to give a breakdown of all your GSCE grades • **Competitions, prizes and master classes**

- **Name your singing teacher** – current and previous (though don't list twenty people here!).

SECTION 2: Performing experience
This should form the other two thirds of your page and should be itemised clearly, in reverse date order. The headings you use will depend on the kind of thing you have done but you could organise them as follows:
- **Solo roles/Chorus**
- **Oratorio/Opera/Recital**
- **School productions/College productions/Professional experience**

There could also be a section for miscellaneous but relevant skills – for example, **languages** (fluent/conversational/basic); **dance; athletic skills; broader musical interests** (jazz/bands/backing vocals/commercial work/film). However you decide to lay it out, keep to a consistent format. For example:

Role • Opera • Venue • Date • Conductor or Director – so
Barbarina • (Le Nozze di Figaro) • Ashton • 1997 • Mark Rondycroft

If you have sung a piece in translation, make it clear. It is important that the eye can see quickly what you have done, so outline the roles in bold for easier assimilation. You must include dates. The panel need to know when you have performed. It is also important to include names of directors and conductors, as it enables the panel to contact their professional colleagues to find out more information about you.

Double and triple check your spellings as roles, places, directors' names, and so on, will NOT COME UP ON A SPELL CHECK! Get somebody else who knows the music world to proof-read your CV for you. You do not want panels to be irritated or distracted by any mistakes.

Biographies

For programmes, you often have to have a short biography. Get used to writing them now, in lengths of between 100 and 250 words. A typical short biography might follow this format:

- 1st sentence – where you were born (date if you are young) and where you were schooled.
- 2nd sentence – musical education teachers/courses/any prizes, and so on.
- 3rd sentence – past experience, mentioning roles/places and directors as for a CV to give the broadest sense of the people you have worked with.
- 4th sentence – this season's performances and future plans.

Obviously, if you are very young and inexperienced, you won't have much to write. **That is fine.** You could include repertoire you have worked on, or are interested in. If you have more experience, aim for concise descriptions of your work. Repeat your name occasionally, rather than using he or she, so that it will 'stick'. Use synonyms rather than always writing 'sang' – for example 'performed', 'appeared', 'took part'. **Make sure you have spelt everyone's name correctly!** You cannot check this too often. Sometimes programme biographies are just abbreviated lists of your work. When going to the theatre or to a concert, look at the programme to get a sense of the different styles used.

Photographs

You will need photographs. Make sure they are a recent likeness and don't overdo the airbrushing – audiences, agents and casting directors need to find you instantly recognisable and memorable from your photo. You may need more than one image. You should have formal and informal shots and you will probably find it helpful to have both colour and black-and-white versions. It is a good idea to store your photos on the computer as well as having hard copies. Always take a copy of your CV and photograph(s) to your auditions.

Being business-like: agents, self-employment and tax

Agents

Agents deal with the business aspect of singing. Whether you are a musical theatre singer or an opera and concert singer, they network for you, negotiate contracts, fees, NAs[3] and in some cases arrange or advise on travel and accommodation. They will deal with enquiries for your services and often send you for auditions. The agent will get feedback from the audition (where possible), which they can pass on to you. This honest exchange is invaluable.

In musical theatre there is also the independent **casting agent**. These people liaise between the production company putting on a show and the theatrical agents who represent individual performers. The casting agent collates vast lists of artists but does not represent them personally.

The normal method of payment to an agent is via a commission on your fee, which can be anything from 10 to 20%. If payment is made directly to the agent, they will take their commission before paying you; if you get the wage, then the agent will bill you. If you are working abroad and another agent has been engaged to negotiate your contract, you should expect to pay both agents, though the percentage will probably be shared.

3 NA = not available. In the professional opera world you may well be able to apply for an NA during the rehearsal period in order to fulfil an engagement elsewhere. The management will reserve the right not to give them, as it will interfere with the scheduling of rehearsals. In musical theatre, NAs are rarely given.

An **exclusive arrangement** with an agent means that they are the only person to represent you; they will expect to take commission on every job, even those you get yourself. You will usually have to get your own work before you can get an agent of any sort. Even if you get representation, don't make the mistake of sitting back, feeling that all the responsibility for finding work has gone to the agent. You must always be active on your own behalf.

Payment, self-employment and tax

 *You should check with the financial representative of the organisation how you will be paid. If you have an agent, the payment may well go directly to them. Sometimes you might find an envelope in your dressing room at the interval. This practice stems from occasions when singers refused to go on for the second half unless they were paid!*

Singers are self-employed – you are running your own *business*. Even if you have an accountant, you **must** keep all your receipts. You will need to keep your contracts and payslips. An accountant does not want to trawl through plastic bags worth of receipts and payslips with no system! The more you order your affairs, the less you will have to pay the accountant.

If working abroad you will need the documentation about the amount of tax you paid in that country (which you will not have to pay again in UK), as well as the details of your expenditure. Have a notebook or some other reliable method of organising information.

In addition, remember that you will be taxed on your *gross* earnings. If you put aside a percentage of your fees the minute you get them, you will always have the money for the taxman. If you put the money into an investment account, you might even make a little profit! You should always account for both the agent's commission and the taxman's quota when working out how much you are earning.

If your performance fee is below a certain level, then you will be paid a weekly rehearsal wage for all the weeks of rehearsal. When you begin performances, this might change into another format but it will all have been made clear in your contract. It may be that you are paid a performance fee but not travel or accommodation expenses. This will mean you have to take advantage of bargain rail tickets or club together with colleagues who have cars. It is all part of the normal experience of a developing professional singer.

Chorus and ensemble in larger companies are usually paid by a weekly wage throughout rehearsal and performance period, with top-ups for understudying and going on. Most contracts have an agreement about the number of rehearsals you can be called for in any given week before being paid any overtime.

Getting a reputation as a reliable artist is essential. The musical and theatrical worlds are small and it is a good thing to develop sound business acumen.

If your performance fee is above a certain level, then you may not be paid any rehearsal fees at all. This can mean that you have four or five weeks without any income. Evidently, this needs good fiscal management. You might be paid in several lump sums – usually the dates will be fixed in your contract. You may well also be able to arrange an advance on your performance fees. If you cancel a performance, you may not get the fee. If you 'walk' the part, and someone else sings it, you will get a percentage of your fee but not the whole thing. All these gradations will be covered in the text of your contract.

5 The last lap

In this section of the book, we will concentrate on:
- Advanced performance.
- Different career paths.

Mary and Tony's handy tips on advanced performance

At this stage in your career you will have trained for a number of years and are looking around for the place where you are most likely to find employment. You need a *niche* and there are several areas of music performance that are specialised. Even if they do not represent the summit of your ambition, you should consider them all. They may serve you well as a stepping-stone to greater things.

Professional chorister

It might be that you have trained for a solo career. However, even if you have a marvellous voice, you may find that you are not suited to the life of a soloist. You may find this life too insecure and that waiting for the next job makes you anxious. You may indeed have responsibilities – mortgages, children, ex-spouses, for example – that make financial security essential. You might not have the 'nerve' for solo singing; in a chorus or ensemble you may feel less exposed and less prone to suffer from your nerves.

For professional choristers employment could be within any of the following:

- Operatic chorus.
- Church choir.
- Professional choir.

Or you could work as an individual session singer.

Operatic chorus

This will require many skills that you already have as an operatic soloist. You will need to have an operatic quality and size of voice. You will have to be able to act, move and be comfortable with props and the demands of a set. You need to have the vocal stamina to endure long hours of strenuous rehearsal. You need to be a good colleague. You will have to be ready to adapt to the ever-changing demands of the director.

The advantage of being in an opera chorus is that you will do many performances; you will also get used to singing in front of an audience and you will be able to observe at close quarters the work of excellent soloists. You will experience great directors and conductors, and sing with a wonderful orchestra. You may not want to stay there forever but you will certainly learn a lot whilst you are there and you will be paid for it. You may even have the opportunity to sing small roles or understudy roles.

Church choir

Church choristers need to be fluent sight-readers, good vocal blenders and have excellent vocal stamina. They need to be able to absorb the music quickly and follow minimal physical instructions from the conductor. They need to be confident and self-reliant. They also need to be good colleagues.

Professional choir

Similar to church choir but professional choristers will sing a wider range of repertoire, from baroque to contemporary. You will have to sing with orchestra and also *a cappella*. Again, you will have to be very skilled at moving between styles and languages, and be a good reader of music. You may tour – either nationally or internationally – and make recordings.

Individual session singer

In this role you are hired as an individual to be part of a group, often for recording purposes. This could involve recording for commercials, or incidental music for film, television or discs. You could be hired to back popular solo singers on television or touring large concert venues. The person who hires is normally called a **fixer**.

You will need to be a good reader and stylistically versatile. You must be very punctual at all times – in this world, time is money! You should expect sessions to come along at very short notice, sometimes even as short as twenty-four hours.

Early music

Early music is a completely generalised term meaning music before (and including) the baroque period. The style is dependent on the dominance of the bass line, usually played on a cello (or period equivalent) with an organ, harpsichord or type of lute playing chords above it. It is generally most appropriate for light, flexible voices.

The consort singer

Before the advent of opera, and the arrival of the *diva* (and *divo*), vocal music was largely performed by groups of singers and musicians. The music could be sacred or secular and accompanied or *a cappella*. Boys were often used for the top line and this has meant that over the last few decades, female singers have been required to sound like boys. Voice types are usually – soprano; second soprano; male alto; tenor; baritone; bass. The mezzo-soprano of nineteenth-century repertoire has almost no place here. Female singers usually have to be able to remove the vibrato from their sound, producing a sound that is sometimes described as 'white'. Controlling the vibrato and making a sound which can blend with others to make a unified whole are essential requirements of the consort singer, whatever their voice type.

You will need to sing exceptionally in tune and be a good sight-reader. Furthermore, the notation may not represent the true pitch that you are singing at, as pitch was not standardised until the nineteenth century and there are many variables to deal with. You will be expected to sing from music that may be notated in a very different way from conventional music and may use some languages in their old forms, for instance, Latin or old French.

The solo singer

Your repertoire might include operas by Monteverdi or Cavalli; songs with lute or other group of instruments; the big solos in church anthems by Purcell; numerous solo cantatas and oratorios. You will have to be vocally flexible and able to execute very fast runs. However short the note, it must be clear and not smudged. There are no *portamenti* in early music. You will have to be able to invent ornamentation appropriate to the style of the music.

Contemporary classical music

This could be described as:

- Music of our own time, written by composers who are alive.
- Music – some of it written in the early years of the twentieth century – which stretches and challenges the singer and the conventions of vocal writing.

It differs from conventional repertoires in the following ways:

- The rhythm might be very complex and bar lengths not regular.
- The harmonic language is rich and possibly atonal.
- The notation may be unfamiliar and original.
- There may be 'effects' written that are not conventional 'singing'.
- You might be required to improvise.

Without doubt, tackling new music will give you skills that you will be able to take into other music. You will learn to hear better and will be quicker at grasping tricky rhythms and harmonies in any conventional score. You will have to make decisions – particularly if working with a living composer on a first performance – about how you are going to execute the piece. You will not be able to rely on recordings or previous performances.

When the notation is unfamiliar and complicated, the task ahead seems daunting. The hardest thing about contemporary music is making the decision to begin work. Once you have understood – at least in theory – what the composer is asking you to do, then you must be brave enough to practise it. The more extreme the demands (and these can be things like laughing or shouting, rather than conventional vocalising), the more you have to try and have a go at them and build up confidence in the new material. As well as conventional use of the singing voice, the singer of contemporary music may be required to do any of the following:

- Heavy breathing.
- Whispering.
- Speaking; declaiming; shouting.
- Singing at the extreme ends of the vocal range.
- Maintaining extremes of tessitura.
- Singing in an over-emphasised vocal colour, not normally associated with classical singing e.g. with no vibrato or a 'breathy' sound.
- Exploring emotional effects and improvising sounds connected with them.

Some composers – Berio for example – also employ sounds that you make with your voice but that are totally unassociated with singing. These techniques are often called 'E.V.T.' or **extended vocal techniques**. What they actually are is perhaps better explained as *everyday* vocal techniques – the sounds that humans make with their voices every day such as snoring, tongue clicking, kissing, blowing raspberries, lip-flutters, and so on.

Some singers maintain that contemporary music is 'bad for the voice' – this is **absolutely NOT true**! This is more likely to be what people say when they are frightened of new styles and unfamiliar sounds. You are far more likely to damage your voice by singing Verdi inappropriately, or before you are ready, than you are by singing this repertoire.

Outreach, education and the community

This is a growing area of work, both nationally and internationally. There are many forums for music and increasingly managers, promoters and funding bodies are looking to find new and exciting places to perform, often with the intention of bringing their work to a wider audience. Most conservatoires have some kind of training programme and many companies – opera companies, theatre companies, orchestras, and so on – have a designated department. This department may be called education or outreach, or it may be named after a person or an idea.

Singers will need to have excellent vocal qualities, sound musicianship, an ability to think on their feet and good and honest, communication. A singer who develops this side of their work will find that it can exist in tandem with other kinds of singing and even bring enhanced strength and performing confidence. Singers may train by going on a course, or by doing a great deal of practical assisting on existing projects. They should apply to the relevant departments for more information about how to proceed.

Animateurs/workshop leaders

The specialists who undertake and lead creative projects – sometimes in schools but also in prisons, homes and many other unusual environments – are usually called animateurs or facilitators. These specialists could be directors, composers, singers, players, dancers or graphic artists, depending on the individual project.

A team leader will be responsible for devising the structure of the project. As well as his or her team of specialists there will also be a junior assistant. Projects are usually managed by a project officer, who is responsible for the administration rather than the creative side. Most animateurs begin with an assistant role, so that they can build up experience without too much pressure and work out their strengths and special areas of interest.

Outreach takes many forms. Work could consist of existing repertoire, newly commissioned repertoire or music and theatre devised by the participants during their sessions. Spaces could be site-specific or theatres, or the open air – almost anything goes. Openness and adaptability is a crucial quality for success in this field.

Concerts and recitals

In an opera, you have days or weeks of rehearsal. As long as you have learned your role, there is time for the fine-tuning of dramatic and musical ideas. Decisions about these are made in collaboration with the director and conductor. You may have several performances and they may each be slightly different.

In concerts (performances with orchestra or small ensemble), you will have to do more preparation on your own. You will have less rehearsal and you may only get one chance to perform the piece. The promoter will have decided on the piece to be performed and will then have engaged the required soloists. In many cases, you should expect to have your major orchestral rehearsal on the afternoon of your performance day.

In recitals (performances with piano or other keyboard, possibly shared with other singers), you will probably have selected the pieces yourself, mostly from the song repertoire. You will be responsible for organising your own rehearsals. The rehearsal on the day may only be to test the acoustic of the hall.

Concerts

You are engaged to sing in a concert. This could be:

- **An oratorio** (for example, Handel's *Messiah*), where there are a number of other soloists.
- **A well-known concert piece** (for example, Mozart's *Exultate Jubilate*), where you are the only soloist.
- **A concert performance of an opera**, where there will be a whole cast of principals but neither set, costumes nor props and where the singers are using the scores, rather than singing from memory.
- **The first performance of a new work**.

In the UK, you may find that you are working for a choral society with an orchestra that is only booked for the day. Therefore, the only complete rehearsal will be on the day of the performance. When employed by a professional orchestra you may have many more rehearsals. In either case, you have to prepare the music well ahead of the performance day. It is very easy to be caught out and find that you have not learned all the music. It is worth checking with the conductor to see which edition of the piece in question they are using. Some editions, for example, may give a movement to the soloists to sing as a quartet that is given to the full choir in other editions.

In oratorio it is usual to sing holding the music, rather than memorising it – you must find a way to use the score without burying your head in it. Practise holding the music in your hands, without using a music stand – you might find the copy a little heavier than you thought! Here are some other things to practise:

- If a piece has different sections, then rehearse them in the right order before the day. Organise a rehearsal with a pianist so you can run through the piece without stopping.
- Experiment with speeds in your own rehearsal time so that you can do whatever the conductor wants.
- Be aware of ensembles, particularly those which are unaccompanied. These can sometimes be difficult to rehearse effectively on your own. Spend extra time on these passages and make sure you are familiar with all the other vocal lines.
- Be prepared for the conductor <u>not to rehearse everything</u>. If your aria is very simple for the orchestra, the conductor may shorten the rehearsal of it.
- Be aware that in performance <u>you</u> are not always the centre of attention! You must learn to be still and focussed when other people are singing.

Concert performance of a show

Sometimes, a company will be presenting something that they have already staged. There might be re-rehearsal to adapt the production to the concert space. Sometimes you will wear your costume, or a simplified version of it. If the performance is a stand-alone event, there are a variety of possibilities for this style of performance:

- **Exactly like an oratorio** – you stay in one position on the stage and sing straight ahead.
- **Modified oratorio** – you make entrances and exits, always standing next to the appropriate character but still singing straight ahead.
- **Quasi-production** – you sing almost from memory and are able to address other characters directly.

The promoter will usually determine the style of the delivery. If this is not the case, discuss ideas with your colleagues. It is possible to 'dress down' from usual concert attire, if this helps the character, but this decision must be taken collectively.

New work

Working on a piece with another musician – usually a keyboard player – in advance of your orchestral rehearsals will enable you to sort out practicalities. Even if orchestral time seems generous, bear in mind that there may be quite a lot of time spent in clarification, or even alteration, of instrumental parts. You must not rely on this time to learn your music!

You may be working with a living composer. If you are uncertain about what they are asking for – in terms of vocal quality or special effect for example – then do not shy from contacting the publisher or composer for clarification. They will be happy to oblige because they want to get the best performance out of you. There may be last minute alterations during the rehearsal stage. Try to be open-minded and adaptable, and do not panic.

Working on new pieces can be the most challenging and satisfying work a singer can do. Grab the opportunity to experience this whenever you can.

Recitals

You may be asked to prepare a recital programme to fit in with a theme already featured or you may be given complete freedom. You will usually be able to choose your own pianist but not always. If the pianist is your regular one, you will know how often you need to meet. If the promoters have fixed the accompanist for you, then rehearsals may be more limited. Enjoy this new musical challenge.

The programme

A good programme has variety of speed, key and mood. It is no longer expected – or even desired – that recitals begin with a group of arie antiche and then progress chronologically until they end with either the 'lighter' repertoire or a token piece of 'modern' music – usually Britten or Walton. Be brave with your repertoire and make some fresh juxtapositions.

Conventionally, an evening recital has a first half of 45 minutes music and a second half of 35. A lunch hour recital will have about 50 minutes of music in it – possibly less. In either case, you must account for the gaps between pieces.

Remember that promoters always ask for *exact* details of your recital a long time before the event. You will need to be precise about theme, content, timings and order. You will probably not be able to change your pieces after the programme has gone to print.

If you have chosen a theme – for instance, songs about spring, love, nature, death or God – first make a list of all the songs you already know which are appropriate. See how many you have. Have you got enough? Is your material all by one composer or all in the same mood? You may need to seek further afield to find pieces to fill the gaps. You might need fast songs or funny lyrics, or if all your songs are short you might need something more substantial (and vice versa).

Once you have the raw material, you will need to decide together how to shape it. This is very labour intensive but brings rich rewards. You need to leave plenty of time to learn the new songs. Ideally, you should determine the programme order *after* you have learned all the material.

In a recital not shared with other soloists, you are likely to have a song-cycle. This is the singer's equivalent of a piano sonata. The composer has determined the order of the songs and their keys. The song-cycle will probably come in the middle of your recital. Since it is the most substantial item, you should determine this first and make the other individual songs fit around it. Apart from the song-cycle, you can group songs in a number of different ways. You may need to juggle them around until you have the best sequence for the songs. You can group songs according to composer or chronologically; you can group by language or theme. You can even mix up the composers, as long as there is some perceivable logic to your decisions. Random selections of the songs you like are not acceptable! A variety of factors will determine your choices:

- **Dramatic:** You want a good range of moods. You don't want four lugubrious songs one after the other and then all the jolly ones together. Creating a world where there is logical dramatic continuity will be more satisfying for an audience. It will also enable you to memorise the material more easily and help you remember the order.
- **Musical:** Try practising the link between one song and another. Sometimes, key-juxtapositions, which at first hearing appear to be startling, can be very

effective. Sometimes, when the song is in the same key as the one before – or when there are many songs in the same key – the effect can be flat and dull. Additionally, remember to mix up fast and slow songs – if you have a great number of fast songs together, the audience can feel breathless; if all the slow ones are together, then you run the risk that the audience will fall asleep!

- **Vocal:** Even though you have all the notes of all the songs, you may find that the order in which you sing them affects how well you can sing them – some people find it hard to sing low songs after high songs, for example. Discover your preferred order by experiment in rehearsal.

Presentation

Performance style in recital is a very personal preference but there are some guidelines. Movement should be minimal but you should not be rigid. Resist wandering around the platform. Gestures should be used with discretion. You should make sure your *voice* is doing the expressing. Beware of raising your arm at the heroic moment or frowning on an expressive chord.

In a dramatic song, like Schubert's *Erlkönig*, you need to explore the best way of presenting the different characters without descending into melodrama. Don't slap on a facial expression ('happy' or 'sad') in order to present a song. If you are inside the text and the music, *thinking* the emotion (which may be 'happy' or 'sad') will produce the right expression on your face. This has been described as **'inside out, not outside in'**.

Be aware of your audience and where they are sitting – you need them all to feel included. Try not to (in cinema parlance) 'pan' them though – looking *everywhere* and yet *nowhere* makes no one feel involved. You should find an appropriate point for your gaze and draw your audience to you.

It is worth checking the lighting in the venue. Ask someone to check that you are standing in a place that shows you at your best. Being out of the light is bad enough but unflattering shadows are even worse!

Of course, there are famous recitalists who break all these 'rules' – who never look at the audience and who are involved in their own private world, on which we, the audience eavesdrop; they walk miles during their performance: little steps back and forward, releasing a frenetic energy. It works for *them*, so don't feel you should copy.

What to wear

Men

There will usually be a dress code for you – tails/ dinner jacket/ lounge suit/ smart-casual – whoever engages you will be able to tell you what is required. In all cases, practise in the clothes you intend to wear. Be comfortable. Make sure that ties and bow ties are not too tight. Cummerbunds may feel restrictive; you must get used to them.

Audiences are often seated beneath you. Make sure trousers and socks are long enough and matching. Shoes should be polished and not look as if you have done the gardening in them. You need to eliminate anything that is distracting when you are seated, as you could be standing and sitting many times. Make sure the trouser pocket linings are the same shade as your trousers.

In a concert, make sure your face is lit so the audience can see all your expressions. People will often think they can't hear you because they can't see you! Girls – be sure that lights behind you do not cause your dress to become transparent!

Wearing your concert clothes, practise sitting and standing whilst holding the music. You should not have to adjust your attire each time.

Women

Finding the right garment to feel good when singing, to blend with another soloist (in style, shape and colour) and to be appropriate for the repertoire being sung is an ongoing challenge. You are on show and you are not static. As you breathe and sing, your body will expand. Practise singing in your concert wear. Make sure it fits. Be aware of slipping shoulder straps, or strapless dresses that travel further south with every breath! Your frock mustn't be the centre of attention. If you have worn it many times, then check it still fits!

When choosing what to wear, bear in mind that the audience may be beneath or above you. Length of hemlines and degree of cleavage can be over exciting when observed from below or above! Make sure you have the right shoes and that you can walk in them.

Women need to bear in mind that they are likely to encounter cold churches or draughts. You need to have a range of clothing suitable for different temperatures. Shawls, whilst bringing warmth, can cause difficulties – because they are not fixed it is hard to manage them whilst holding the music. Work out a way of securing them safely and unobtrusively, so that you have freedom of movement.

When singing with other soloists, if it is practicable, discuss what to wear. Be a good colleague. Think about colour, shape and style. If consultation is impractical, then taking two dresses along is a good idea. Helping the audience with the character you are playing – even in oratorio – is important. For example, the Angel in Elgar's *The Dream of Gerontius* is unlikely to wear a skimpy, strapless, red number – even if it is your favourite dress!

For recitals, almost anything goes. Fashions have changed and tails/ ball gowns are no longer de rigueur. Lunchtime recitals tend to be more informal than evening ones.

If you are working abroad then get advice about usual customs for clothing.

Building stamina

You have to be responsible for the building of your stamina. You should prepare your music well in advance – security of the notes and the text is only part of the job. You need to have 'sung in' the piece thoroughly. This is something that is taken for granted in opera and is a natural result of the repetition of rehearsal, which is not provided for you in concert work.

You also have to make sure that you have the stamina to sing through the piece twice on the same day, if that is going to be required. You may have to 'mark' in the rehearsal in order to give your best performance to the paying audience. **Marking is a very advanced skill.** If you simply constrict your throat in an attempt to mark, you will do more harm than good. It is better to sing out. Even when marking you must give an accurate performance, though you can save your energy and power. The choir and orchestra need to hear clear cues and the conductor must feel confident that you know the piece. For successful marking, your energy will be distilled and intensified. The text and the rhythm must be vividly delivered. You can drop high notes down the octave and come off the voice on any long notes. You may want to sing out in tricky transitional passages.

Preparing for the stage

It is the goal of every performer to give a truthful and believable performance, whether you are singing opera or musical theatre. Some people are 'stage animals' – without any particular training they just know what to do. Most people, however, require some instruction and everybody can hone their stage skills.

As an advanced singer, you will have, even if only fleetingly, the 'out of body' experience when your singing is effortless and carefree. You feel carried along by the wave of music and hardly conscious of yourself at all. You are aiming to perform with an illusion of total abandon. Things are, of course, rehearsed but the audience must feel that everything is spontaneous. However, if you always lose yourself in the music, you might not achieve your dramatic potential.

A singer needs to be extremely self-aware. This will already be obvious to you from your first lessons. When you reach performance – and particularly performance for the stage – there are things beyond vocal and musical issues that you need to conquer. Arms, hands, feet, movement, dancing, prop handling, costume wearing, and so on, now come into the frame. Your *whole body* will express the character that you are playing. In exploring these new skills, it is often the case that you may temporarily lose some of your vocal competence. You are adding new layers, bit by bit, and must therefore make a conscious and confident decision to let go of technical concerns. You must free up your brain to respond to new challenges.

Active neutral

Most directors will at some point talk about the **neutral state**. In order to understand this concept, we could take the analogy of a painter's blank canvas, ready to be painted on. The blank canvas can be equated with a 'neutral' state. You must begin with yourself and appraise how you look and appear. What is your habitual expression? Do you always smile? Does your face, in repose, look sullen or glum? You may have to ask your friends! In playing another character, you may have to become a little less 'yourself'.

The neutral state must not make you vacant (unless of course this is a feature of the character you are playing). You must be in a state of readiness – alert, ready to go but not over-excited. When you find this, you have found an **active neutral** state. This that will be useful to you in all singing, whether it is on stage or not. It will give you a solid base and enable you to find effective and economical methods of expression.

Learning to be direct and truthful

Before you can be truthful as another character, you have to engage in some un-blinkered self-assessment. You need to approach the following exercises with great honesty. You may have to *re-learn* to look – you must stand back a little from your self. Remember that in the end, self-awareness is not necessarily self-criticism.

- Introduce yourself with your name – spoken naturally – into a full-length mirror, as if the reflection was another person. Do it clearly and plainly, without apologising in any way. Apologies can be conveyed subliminally in many subtle ways – a little 'tic', a cough, a giggle, a shrug. You may not be aware of the message you are sending out. Be observant.
- Sing to yourself in the mirror. Keep your eyes open, remembering to be ruthless in looking at your eyes and not somewhere about the chin.
- Perform a song or aria into the mirror. Can you notice any repeating tics? For instance, do you: raise your eyebrows when you breathe? Fiddle with your fingers? Lift one shoulder higher than the other? Swing your hips? Close your eyes between phrases or on high notes? Demonstrate the contours of a musical phrase with your arms? Accompany the most important note or word in a phrase with a gesture that emphasises the meaning of the word? Try the song again and see if you can eliminate these.

You might feel that by successfully removing all your tics you will become inexpressive and un-committed. This is only a passing stage and it is worth persevering to eliminate casual and imprecise movements that do not add anything to your singing and which take up valuable neurological space that could be better used. Tics are distracting – audiences can become riveted by watching your fidgeting fingers, for example. If you cannot eliminate them, you might inadvertently carry them into a new character that you are playing. If you don't succeed, then keep at it. Some people have good control over involuntary movement and some people have to work harder at it. Try not to fall in love with your own tics. Do not say 'oh yes, I know I do that' as if it was a badge of pride. You will not lose your individuality! If you find that your tics recur, try this extra exercise:

- Try extending the small movement into a large one. Make it huge – thus a finger fiddle becomes something that goes into the whole arm; an eyebrow lift is taken into the whole upper body. For shoulders, press them down equally with your hands. For swaying hips, make huge hip swivelling circles. If the swaying is in arms, then turn them into big torso movements.
- Make the gestures really big.
- Try walking around the room using these bigger movements.
- After this, try to settle again and see if it is easier to be still.

Now, conscript a friend to help you in your work. This friend can assist you in your search for self-awareness – they can help you look more honestly at what you are doing. It is important to stress that this should be a person who you can really trust. Perhaps you can have a reciprocal arrangement with another singer. In order to be comfortable and fluent on stage, you must be able to conquer pride and the fear of looking foolish. Working with a friend can give you lots of trial runs at performance and raise your levels of confidence.

Try the following exercises together:

- *Sing a song or aria in performance mode, standing and looking directly into your friend's eyes, without closing your own. Can you hold their gaze without glazing over?*
- *Try sitting opposite your friend who is also seated. Sing your piece again as if you were chatting to them in a café. What do you notice?*

The second part of the exercise will involve the asking and answering of questions. The friend has looked you with honest and non-judgemental appraisal. The question you ask should not be about your singing, for example:

- *Was I any good?*
- *Did you like that high note?*

But only about simple objective fact, for instance:

- *Did my eyebrows move?*
- *Did I lift my eyebrows when I sang the high note?*

In the second exercise, there may be feedback from you to the friend, as your piece and your singing may feel quite different when performed in a more conversational or 'natural' manner.

Working on a character

Understanding and building a character is a vital part of the singer's toolbox. This skill is relevant to all singing, whatever the style. You will probably have already been encouraged to think about character when learning songs. When you are singing in the theatre, it will be a great advantage to be able to have an opinion about your character that goes beyond the text that you sing. You need, in other words, to have contextual or background information.

All audiences want to see something believable. You must construct a logical chain of behaviour. You will need to look at the emotional journey that a character goes on. In theatrical music, you should be aware of the state of mind of a character at every juncture of the music that they sing and even when they are off stage and not singing. It is also good to be aware of what has happened to them before the piece starts – if you have the information from the plot that is easy but sometimes you may need to construct something for yourself. It can also be fun to think about what happens – or might happen – to the character after the piece is over.

Researching the character: getting the facts

You need to read the whole libretto or script, not just your part! Accumulate as many pieces of information as you can. In order to fully understand the plot, you may need to do some research on the background to the opera or show.

What have you found out about your character? Their age, gender, class, experience, are they in love or not, for example? Can you find a hundred statements about them, or only six? What has happened to this person before the action begins? What happens to them between scenes? Who do they meet in the story? Is there anyone they never meet? What do they feel about all the other characters they meet?

Try to stay in the first person i.e. *I* do this … or *I* said to Fred and not *he/she* does … or *he/she* said … and so on. This will prevent you from judging your character. Points like 'she's a trollop' or 'he's really stupid' keep you at a distance from the character you are playing. Now you can:

- Write a list of all the things you say about yourself (as your character). Keep these factual.
- Make a list of all the things other characters say about you.

After making these lists, do another exercise:

- Write down how do you feel about these statements made by other characters. Are they all true?
- Now, write down how you feel about the other characters.

As you do more preparation, you will realise that although the text provides some undisputed facts, you will have to supply some things from your imagination in order to flesh out a character. This is particularly true if your character is a small part. Some things can be open to interpretation. Rehearsals may well involve experimentation to find the best way to present individuals and the relationships between them. Ultimately, the director should guide you into selecting the best of your options.

The text

As discussed earlier, text work away from the music is invaluable. You must be emotionally alive when you are not actually singing! Long introductions or postludes must be a reflection of your state of mind, not merely a moment or two for you to gather your technical thoughts, get settled in a chair, climb steps, and so on. Try to imagine what the character is thinking when they are not singing. Speak some of these thoughts aloud.

Are you aware where there are shifts in the text and the music that take you in a new emotional direction? These can also be called 'thought changes'. You will sometimes find easy clues in the text to help you mark them out. One straightforward example is the word 'but'. For example: you might be going along happily singing about the love you have for your husband. Then along comes a sentence that reads; 'but my father is his enemy' and then you go on to describe the love you have for your father. These two statements show the character in conflict. Here, the word 'but' indicates the precise moment of that thought change.

For musical theatre and operatic shows with dialogue, you have to find clear reasons why your character goes from speech into song. There will be a 'lift-off' moment. In general, the sung passages are at a higher emotional dynamic than the spoken passages. You will need to practise in order to move seamlessly – from a technical point of view – from speech to song.

Repeats

If you are singing an aria that has a da capo section or a musical theatre number with many verses, can you vary the emotional tone so that you are propelled on a forward journey?

Remember that there is no going back in a live performance. You should think of repeats as a fresh look at the text, with extremely similar musical material. In opera in particular, there are many repeats of the same words using identical music. In musical theatre, you are more likely to encounter different text to the same music.

If you have to repeat a word or phrase, then try to work out *why* you do – *why* does the character repeat? Is it because they are not getting what they want and they have to re-emphasise their desire? Or, are they suddenly unconfident? Do they have some kind of sudden revelation, which causes them to reflect further on the statement they have just made? It is not enough to say; 'I'll do this again, louder'. You must have a reason, beyond something that is musically satisfying. *Louder* and *softer* should be seen as manifestations of an emotion. For example, you feel suddenly triumphant and if you allow yourself to experience this emotion, then the dynamic will be louder. You are trying to connect your musical choices to the appropriate feelings of the character.

Communicating your decisions

There is a difference between an intellectual understanding of a character's development and the confident physical portrayal of that understanding on stage. After doing your research, and some practical exercises, you are ready to put your performance 'on its feet'. So far, you have been sitting, or standing. You have not yet moved about! The days are long gone when a singer could just stand and sing, and impress everyone with the beauty of his or her voice.

Physical confidence

Your physical confidence will improve with use and understanding of your body.

Whatever your shape and size, you must be able to convey physical confidence. Directors who have come from the theatre world expect opera singers nowadays to be willing to experiment with physical movement. Musical theatre singers, often from a dance background, will already have had the importance of movement drilled into them.

> • Raise your level of **fitness**. If not down at the gym, then walk, jog, or swim. Singing is an athletic activity, whatever your theatrical genre. You need to be strong and healthy to avoid coughs and colds.
> • Do some form of activity that increases your **flexibility** – perhaps yoga, shiatsu or Alexander technique.
> • Do some form of activity that increases your **physical co-ordination** skills – tap dancing, salsa, flamenco, racquet sports, for instance.
> • Learn how to **relax and wind down**. Learn how to clear your mind. Yoga, meditation, cooking, gardening, reading, or other similar activities can help.

You must be able to sing when carrying out all kinds of different tasks. You have to manage props and costumes. You have to find your light. You have to be able to follow a conductor with your peripheral vision. You will have to be able to do this whatever the demands of the production. Imagine this 'worst case scenario':

> You are coming onto the stage down some stairs wearing a long cloak. There is a blinding light in your eyes. The steps are uneven and the treads are narrow. You have a wide-brimmed hat on and you are carrying a guitar ready to play. Both hands are therefore occupied and you cannot use them to help you with the cloak. You have your eyes glued to your beloved, who is downstage. Furthermore, you are a person of very high status, so looking down, or tripping up, is not an option! On top of all this, which is already difficult to execute without disaster, you must at all times be mindful of the conductor, so that you don't lose your place in the music!

This is an extreme case but not beyond the bounds of possibility. How can you learn to cope with these demands? You can use your own home environment to prepare for the theatrical one. Try the following:

> - Sing through an aria or number moving (stamping or walking on the spot) in time with the pulse of the music.
> - Keep singing at the right speed but move at double; half; triple speed.
> - In a big space, do the same thing travelling forward. Cover big distances. Keep your eyes focussed on a point straight ahead of you. Don't look at your feet!
> - Sing an aria or number and go through a regular pattern of moves e.g. stand; sit; pick up something; put it down – and then repeat. Sing at normal volume.
> - Sing through the piece and perform a rhythmically **unstructured** activity e.g. lay the table; wash the bath; tidy your wardrobe and so on. It is important that you do not mark or croon.
> - Lie on your back on the floor. Sing your piece and as you do so get up to a standing position. Try this in as many different ways as you can.
> - Practise these exercises in different clothes – long, short, tight, loose and in different footwear from none at all, right through to high heels. Boys – you too may have to wear heels from time to time!

As a general principle, 'mark' these exercises through first and as you acquire more confidence, move into singing out fully. Assess how all these different things affect your singing. You are trying to improve your co-ordination and your ability to multi-task – all crucial skills for the stage performer. Do not, however, make these tasks so hard that you risk injury or force your voice.

Focus and individuality

A performer has to be aware that 'focus' doesn't mean glazed over or 'fixed'. All performances have to have inner life. Singers often fall into the trap of being so poised that they are conveying no personality at all. The singer's imagination is a vital tool. What makes for differences in singer's performances is often to do with this quality, more than technical competence, vocal excellence or musical ability.

Singers often think that they have to do everything *right*. As we have already seen, there is a lot of 'right' to do. You are bombarded with information and instruction, and you try to do it all. However, whatever the instructions you have had, at some point you must make the piece your own. You shouldn't just be making pallid copies of other people's performances. Try the following exercises to help with focus and imagination:

- Sing an aria or number looking at someone. Start close up and then gradually move further and further away from each other. Don't close your eyes.
- Imagine that you have two people in front of you, one to your left and one to your right. Sing your piece making contact with these imaginary people alternately. Never drift in between them in 'no-man's land'.
- Keeping these two 'people', imagine that you hate one and love the other. Sing your piece using these emotions to colour the alternate phrases. Don't try and attach the meaning of the song to the emotions. You are doing this to explore vocal colour!
- Do the same exercise as above trying other opposing emotions or states (fun – fear; tickle – scratch; seduce – terrify; lull to sleep – issue orders). Some of these will stretch your imagination more than others.
- Visualise an image in front of your eyes. It can be related to the context of your piece but it doesn't have to be. Sing your piece and keep your eye on this image. As you continue to sing, the first picture can change to another picture, as if you were watching a slide show. Sing throughout as if you were commenting on or describing the pictures you see in front of you.
- If your song is about passionate love, try to think of some physical sensations that correspond to that word. 'Love' might make you feel full of breathless excitement or feverish anticipation, for example. Now sing but think only of these physical sensations. The singing is the sensation.

You will notice things about your voice when you do these exercises. Perhaps the top feels freer; perhaps you barely notice your technical anxieties; perhaps you get really engrossed in the world of the imagination. This concentrated energy is very compelling in a performer.

Conclusions

On the one hand, learning how to sing well is a very rigorous activity. There are numerous skills to acquire, develop and hone. You must be methodical in your preparation. On the other hand, at the moment of delivery – that is, the performance – you must exude enjoyment, spontaneity and freshness. All singers need to strive to find the right balance between these two contrasting factors.

It might be true to say that the thing that marks out a *great* performer, is not what they do the *same* as everyone else but what they do *differently*. This is very elusive and, of course, also subjective. However, if you can be in free and creative contact with your imagination, not only in practice time but also in the moment of performance, you may well be able to access this special 'x' factor!

6 The home straight

In this section of the book, we will concentrate on:
- Success.
- Practice and self-discipline.
- Consequences of auditions.
- The singer's job.

Success: what does it take?

So far we have offered some guidance on some of the key aspects of a performer's training. We have been considering what each singer is likely to encounter as they progress along their chosen path. In the main, we have been dealing with what other people will supply for the singer and how the singer reacts to all of the information that they receive; how they must process it effectively in order to keep moving forward. Now we discuss the things that singers must be responsible for themselves, without external help – you could call this *inner strength*. The list of qualities a singer needs in order to have a chance of success is as follows:

- A good and technically fluent voice.
- Musicianship.
- Linguistic skill.
- Acting ability.
- Health and stamina.
- Powers of concentration.
- A resonant speaking voice.
- Good physical co-ordination and the ability to move well.
- Good communication.
- Casting appeal.
- The ability to make the most of their appearance.

There are two factors that we have left off this list – commitment and resilience. We will now analyse how these particular factors manifest themselves.

Practice and self-discipline

Firstly you have to crack the business of practice. If you would always rather be reading a book, chatting to friends or having a cup of coffee, you will not progress! The only person who can do the practice is you and you must learn not to put off *starting* it. No matter how brilliant your teacher, and your lessons, *you* have your voice and no one else does – **nobody can do your work for you!**

Of course, you have to know *what* to do in your practice and your teacher will advise you. Many people make the mistake of thinking that clocking up hours is enough. It is *how* you practise that determines its efficacy. You will need to be persistent when it seems that progress is slow and difficult. It is easy to be downhearted. It is also vital to know when you should *not* practice – when you are sick, exhausted or even when you are over-emotional. By over-emotional we mean stressed, grief-stricken, panic-stricken, angry – anything which disturbs your equilibrium. Of course, it is important to feel these emotions rather than deny them and different people respond to them in different ways. Be sensitive to what works for you.

*There is a famous adage that declares: if you don't practise for one day, **you** notice; if you don't practise for two days, **your critics** notice; if you don't practise for three days, **the audience** notices.*

The most effective practice happens with a clear head. Panic about how little time you have can be a useful motivator … but the practice *itself* should be calm! Don't forget that learning how to be self-motivated is, however, part of your job. Be curious about all the arts. Go to concerts, opera, theatre and dance. Hear young singers at the music and drama colleges. Stimulate your mind. Listening only to recorded voices gives a limited perspective on singing. It may give a false impression of the ease of a piece – perhaps it took fifty takes! Maybe a breath was edited out or a top note inserted! Singing for recordings and singing live are two separate phenomena – hear both.

You can also learn from musicians who are not singers. Many fine instrumentalists go to hear good singing in order to learn about legato and liquid phrasing. Reciprocally, singers can learn about style, musicianship and tonal colour.

Auditions and the consequences

You have started to audition. You go off to sing and are either happy with the way it has gone, or you feel it has gone badly. What happens next might not correspond to how you felt the audition had gone:

- You are contacted and offered the role you wanted.
- You are offered a role that you weren't going for or expecting.
- You are offered something that you don't want to do or don't think suitable.
- You are contacted with a personal letter saying the organisation has nothing for you at the moment but requesting that you keep in touch with them.
- You get a standard letter, thanking you for coming but offering you nothing.
- You get a letter saying you should not give up your day job!
- You never hear anything from the organisation at all.

How do you deal with all those things? If you want the job and are free, you say yes. If there are problems with the dates, then you have to decide how to negotiate your diary with the parties concerned.

It is difficult to know how you come over in audition. You might think of yourself as a lyric tenor and have dreams of singing Rodolfo in Puccini's *La Bohème*; the panel may feel that you would be better suited to character parts. You have a choice here, of course, and no one can force you to do parts you don't want to. However, the panel may be right. Give the matter some thought. If you are offered a lesser role than the one you hoped for, or an understudy, you may be hugely disappointed. Don't react too quickly and wait till you have got over your disappointment before responding. Discuss the options with your teacher and colleagues. You want to avoid shutting a door irrevocably.

If an organisation is interested in you but has no immediate work for you, then you just have to remember to keep them informed of what you are doing. Sometimes they will tell you when they want to hear you again but not always.

The standard letter – polite and noncommittal – is hard to accept. Try not to dwell on it. Develop a 'win some, lose some' attitude. If you get a letter that is very negative in tone, then ask yourself if you are singing the right repertoire. Do you send the right signals about the kind of person you are? You must do enough auditions to 'test drive' your pieces and discover how they work under pressure. Many organisations are overloaded with administrative duties and simply do not contact you after your audition. This does not necessarily mean your audition was bad.

Some general points

Feedback

Feedback of any sort, either written or verbal, is difficult to give and receive. Unless someone on the panel can give you a significant amount of time in which to discuss your audition, feedback can backfire. The panel only hear you for a short time and have to judge you very quickly. They perhaps don't know enough about your performing history to know whether this has been a fair representation of you. However, if you know someone on the panel – and they know your singing – then that person can be a useful barometer for you. There is no requirement that an audition panel give feedback and increasingly they do so less and less.

Casting decisions

Some casting decisions are made not on what you sound like, or even what you look like, but on something so nebulous and subjective that it is hard to describe at all, let alone write about. Call this 'personality', 'energy', 'essence' or 'spirit' – all of these words hold something of the truth. A casting panel might say something like 's/he just doesn't *feel* right for the role'. You may have been the 'best' singer but still not get the role because the director is looking for something particular – age, height, style, for instance. In the world of musical theatre casting, the director has even more say than in the classical field. Mezzos or 'belters' may have a problem in their twenties when they are simply the wrong playing age for the roles that suit them vocally.

Your own evaluation

When you get a good result you will try to work out what you did in the audition so that you can repeat the formula to get more jobs. But, mystifyingly, you will soon discover that sometimes you sing badly and get a job, and sometimes you sing well and do not. You can only perform what you have prepared to the best of your ability. All panels' opinions are subjective.

Another possibility is that someone on the panel promises you a job in the audition itself. You leave the room on cloud nine, thinking the best job of your life is in the bag. However, you hear nothing at all, until you notice a flyer for the job in question with *another singer's name* on it. Sadly, the enthusiastic panellist may not have had all the facts and not have enough power to deliver the promise, *and* was premature in their praise.

To conquer disappointment, you will need resolve. You must learn not to take setbacks personally. All you can do is sing your best, try to treat the audition as a performance, and *enjoy* it. Remember that the job you are going for is not the only job in the world.

Networking and getting along with your colleagues

Many of the best jobs come serendipitously – you don't really know how it happened but you were just in the right place at the right time. It follows that you have to be in *some* place though – being locked away at home won't help you. You have to find a way to get out and about, and amongst the people who are in the business. You hear about auditions and performances from your colleagues. You may meet people socially before you actually work with them. Your ability to get on with them is important – you might meet them later in a working environment and you don't want to start off on the wrong foot.

Theatre and music are essentially team efforts. The success of any theatrical or musical venture is dependent on the way *each* of the component parts is working. You have to learn to get along with people. They don't have to be your best friend but you have to be able to co-exist with them over the course of a rehearsal and performance period.

Doing the job

When you rehearse there are many people to satisfy:

- The **coach and répétiteur** will be expect you to be accurate to the written page and sing in tune with clear diction.
- The **language coach** will expect you to be faithful to the text and accurate with pronunciation.
- The **conductor** will have strong views about the interpretation of the music.
- The **director** will have a clear view of the drama and expect you to fit into his or her concept.
- The **choreographer** will expect you to be able to move with fluency and pick up steps quickly (and without forgetting to sing!).
- The whole **stage management** team who are in charge of the running of the rehearsal.
- Your **colleagues** in the cast with whom you will collaborate.
- **Yourself** – you may be the hardest taskmaster of all.

A lot of information will be thrown at you. You will process what you can and add layers as you gain in confidence. It is quite normal for words and music to disappear out of your head when you add production or choreography. **Assuming you have prepared properly**, you should not despair. Never worry about making mistakes – you must try things out. This is why the process is called a rehearsal!

Don't get a reputation for lateness. Not only does it irritate the stage management but it also infuriates your colleagues. Learn to be punctual.

There will always be a lot of sitting around, as you wait for your scene. Find something constructive to do to stop getting bored. You could:

- Memorise the next scene, or write moves of the last one in your score.
- Do some embroidery or tapestry.
- Do a crossword.
- Watch the rehearsal.

Less good ways of occupying yourself include:

- Phoning your friends on your mobile.
- Chatting with the cast about how terrible the production is.
- Reading a novel that is so absorbing that you get totally lost in it.
- Falling asleep somewhere where the stage management can't find you.

Répétiteur
(from the French 'la répétition', meaning rehearsal) – a rehearsal pianist who is an invaluable stand in for the orchestra. They have to play for all the production and stage rehearsals and can become an important support for you. If asked, they may give you very helpful advice or an impartial opinion about your singing.

The conductor and the director

You need to put them at their ease by demonstrating that you are punctual, well prepared and reliable. Remember that first impressions count.

Usually, before the production rehearsals begin, there will be a period of time set aside to work on the music alone. You should ensure that you are *very* well prepared for the first working session with the conductor. Your contract will usually have a clause stating that you must know your music when you arrive. If you are not prepared, then the organisation is under no obligation either to employ or to pay you.

The conductor may tell you bluntly that you are not singing in tempo, in tune or responding to a cue, and so on. Try not to take this personally! Do not sulk or look for defensive excuses. Do not blame your colleagues, your singing teacher or coach. The best solution is to try again and correct your mistake without any argument.

Some directors have a clear 'map' of the production before they start and organise proceedings in accordance with that map. Many more directors have a fluid approach to their work and will, as a matter of course, experiment as they go along. They have a clear 'view' but not a 'map'. In this case, you should remain as open to their suggestions as you can. The director is the only person who can see things from the audiences' point of view. In other words, they have a better idea of whether their vision for the piece is coming over the footlights successfully. They have to be allowed to change their mind if things are not working. This can be frustrating! In the musical theatre world, where new pieces are premiered weekly, performers have to get used to rewrites and long extra rehearsals.

Some directors work with the text in an improvisatory way, so it is a good idea to prepare the text a little without its music. Some directors do exercises or 'theatre games' as a method of getting to know a group and building solidarity within the company.

Stage management

The stage management role is to provide the link between the artistic and technical departments. They make sure that everyone knows all of the requirements of the different elements of the production – for example, they give timings to the wardrobe department for quick changes; they tell the props department what is needed, and so on. They make sure that the rehearsals run smoothly. They mark up the outline of the set on the floor and make sure that complicated pieces of scenery are well represented (e.g. doors, windows, stairs). They ensure that all of the props are available for use. Props can change as the rehearsal progresses. A 'stand in' might be used until the right thing is ready. Be flexible if you can. They ensure that rehearsals start on time and that everyone who is called is present. Their role is to make everything onstage work while keeping life as comfortable for you as possible. Whilst they will do everything they can to help you, resist the temptation to treat them as servants!

The choreographer

The choreographer will come into the production calls according to the needs of the particular show. If there is a large dance component, you will sometimes be provided with a class but mostly you should be responsible for your own physical warm-up. Be aware that strenuous movement without limbering up can cause damage.

In opera, there may only be a few chances to work on the choreography *with* the choreographer and you may have to be responsible for drilling the steps yourself. You will almost certainly have to do some homework to allow you to sing and move at the same time!

In dance-led shows in musical theatre, the dance calls will be daily and elaborate. Musical theatre singers learn which shows call for dancer-singers, rather than singer-movers.

Rehearsal etiquette

Resist the impulse to talk about members of the cast in public places and don't offer advice to a fellow performer, unless asked for it. If you ask what someone is being paid for a job, be prepared to feel glum if they turn out to be being paid more than you are for the same job.

There are certain etiquettes to be observed if you are involved in stage kissing. Fresh breath; no garlic! If you have a cold, 'mark' the kissing rather than infect your colleague. Unless you have permission, do not stick your tongue down your colleague's throat!

Try to maintain your own focus and space without infringing on that of your colleagues. If you are sharing a dressing room, be sensitive to others. Loud warming up and constant talking can be hard to ignore.

Almost all singers are given to whining and whingeing when things get changed! **Try not to be one of those singers!** Be a problem solver and not a problem finder. In all cases, try out the suggestions of the director, conductor, or designer before raising objections.

Understudies/covers

Understudying can be very frustrating but think of it as a wonderful opportunity to prepare a role and to be coached in it, and to observe more experienced artists at close quarters. As understudy you need to be aware that because of time limitations, you have to be more resourceful and thorough in preparation. You could also be in the show doing chorus or a small part and covering a larger role. This means that you will probably watch scenes and make notes from the wings. Bear in mind that in new productions at least, the understudies don't always get a lot of rehearsal before the show is actually up and running. Although you may never go on, be as prepared as you can be as you may find yourself on stage on the first night!

In musical theatre, there may be two covers for each main role and one cover that may even sing a role once or twice a week. If you are in the ensemble of a long-running show, you may well be required for rehearsals when there are cast changes on top of your eight shows in the week! If you are the only person new to a long-running show, you may have very little opportunity to rehearse with the whole cast. The task of 'swing' is particular to musical theatre, when one person takes on a number of smaller roles and covers them all.

Costume and make up

You will have had a fitting, probably quite early on. It may be that everything is straightforward and your costume is 'right' first time. However, you may not like the costume and feel it does nothing for your looks and confidence. This can be a vulnerable time for a performer. Negotiating change is a delicate operation. Sometimes there is flexibility and sometimes not. There is no harm in discussing your costume with the person who is actually designing it.

When you start to get into costume and wigs, be prepared for some slight adaptations to the production. Although you may well have had appropriate rehearsal wear, some costumes are harder to get used to than others. They may oblige you to move, sit and stand differently; they might take up more space on stage.

Sometimes make up will be done for you and sometimes you will responsible for it yourself. If there is a particular look, then you may well be provided with a chart or guide to copy. Practise at home!

Quick changes are an art. You must learn, in all probability, to stand still and let the dresser do their job. If you panic, everything will be worse.

Wigs can come off and false moustaches develop a life of their own. Hair gets stuck in lipstick, hats with large brims mean you cannot see the conductor, helmets mean you can't hear a thing. Swords bump into your colleagues. Long trains on skirts and cloaks can cause havoc when going up and down stairs. Leather-soled shoes slip when you make a quick entry. Corsets and tight-fitting garments can feel very restrictive – you need to become accustomed to them.

Lighting

Modern lighting designs are very sophisticated. Lighting may come from the wings as well as the front of the stage. When you are *in* the light, you will be able to feel it on your eyelashes. A performer has to be aware of light on other singers, as well as themselves. It is very easy to lose concentration and not realise that you are standing in a cross light which is the only illumination for a colleague.

Pressures of rehearsing

As a rule, 'stage-and-piano' rehearsals are managed by the director and 'stage-and-orchestra' rehearsals by the conductor. Generally speaking, rehearsals start optimistically though as the performance approaches, the pressure rises! The conductor or director may make more demands on the performer. At this point, singers might become insecure. They might indeed, get ill, as they try to deal with the extra demands of the stage rehearsals.

Directors sometimes get short-tempered as they deal with the technical requirements – quick set changes, complex lighting cues and so on. The singer may not always be the main focus of attention. Avoid arguing with the conductor or director in public, especially in front of the orchestra or chorus. This doesn't mean that you can never raise your point of view; it just means that you should choose your moment wisely. Try not to hold up expensive rehearsal time.

When things are repeated, don't assume it's always because of you! It may be to do with the practicalities of the set, or lights or even props. It may be to do with speeds that need adjusting now the full orchestra is playing; it may be that the balance needs re-thinking. If you know that a section is being repeated for stage or technical reasons, then you will probably be able to mark. If there is a balance issue, then the conductor will ask you to sing out. Remember that you may have to 'cheat' some of the scenes in order to be heard against the orchestra in a big space. It may not be possible to sing directly upstage, for example, or straight across the stage.

As first night approaches, concentrate on your own job, rather than worrying about other people and their jobs. However, become hyper-aware of **health and safety**. When people are tired and fractious, accidents can happen. Stages are dangerous places!

Discipline in the wings is crucial. Be prompt and quiet – noisy behaviour is distracting for your fellow performers onstage and irritating for the technical staff. It is also surprising how much offstage noise an audience can hear.

Whatever the situation, make sure you treat everybody – your colleagues, crew, lighting, stage management, dressers – with respect. If you are civil to them, they will do anything to help you.

After the performance

You have got through the show – well done! There has been applause and much excitement. How might you feel?

- Thrilled that you have accomplished everything you hoped for.
- You can't wait for the next performance and to have that feeling again.
- Unhappy that you have made vocal or musical 'mistakes'.
- Exhausted.
- Desolate and inconsolable.

After a good performance, euphoria is normal. You may find that your adrenaline level is so high that you can't 'come down' for hours. If you think it didn't go well, perhaps it was not as bad as you thought. A mistake that felt huge to *you* might have been barely noticeable to anyone else.

In the 'green room' your public awaits. They might be friends, or your colleagues' friends, or critics. You may well feel very vulnerable and emotional after a show and it may be hard to meet some of these people.

You have to develop mental strength to cope with some of the comments you will hear. People can say some odd things and we give you below a few we have heard (the italics represent the things that you would sometimes like to retort but usually don't!):

- 'I liked your dress!'   *(But what about my singing?!)*
- 'I see your technique is holding up.'   *(Excuse me???)*
- 'I never realised the role was so difficult.' *(He thinks I was awful.)*
- 'Wasn't Susan marvellous?'   *(What about me?)*
- 'God, I hate that piece!'   *(But did you like me?)*
- 'Have you heard from Henry?'   *(Who's Henry? Did you like the show?)*
- 'That dress didn't fit very well.'   *(Oh God, I looked a pudding. I told the designer I would!)*
- 'Have you got a cold?'   *(NOOOOO …)*

- 'Gosh, that was a bad moment when you fell over.'   *(That was in the production!)*

Sometimes, depending on who makes the comment, you can say what you really feel. Sometimes it's easier to deflect discussion and defer it to another day. Many singers choose to make polite excuses – for instance saying that they have a performance the next day and need an early night – and make a quick getaway.

Next morning

There may be reviews – some singers choose never to read them; some read them after the run of performances is over; some go out and buy every one they can find. Sometimes, even if you try to avoid them, a friendly soul will tell you the contents. It is very hard to avoid hearing about spectacularly bad reviews or real raves. Only with experience will you know how you want to deal with them. A bad review can disturb and undermine the confidence of the performers. It can even cause tension in the cast if acclaim or censure goes to one particular person. Remember, that critics have to put in their copy quickly and they won't necessarily be giving a considered judgement. There might also have been editorial cuts for which they were not responsible. Their opinion is subjective in any case.

Reflection

After the run of performances you will need to have a 'post-mortem':

- Were you voiceless after the first night, and if so, were you 'punching above your weight'?
- Did the shows get easier as you went along?
- How did you manage your stamina?
- Did you feel that some shows were better or fresher than others? Do you know why?
- What can you learn that you can put into practice the next time?
- Was there anything about your colleagues or about the rehearsal process that you would deal with differently another time?
- What did you learn about the character? Was there anything that occurred to you mid-performance that would make you approach the role completely differently the next time you do it?
- Did you find it easy to bond with people in the show? Are *you* easy to get on with?

Assessment and consultation

If you are attempting to perform professionally rather than just for pleasure, it may be helpful to put down a few markers:

- *Set yourself goals – short, medium and long term. Make sure that they are realistic by consulting with your teachers and coaches.*
- *If you are persistently going for auditions that you fail to get, have an honest appraisal with your teachers and coaches.*
- *Try not to blame other people for your failures.*

A fine singer did her debut recital at the Wigmore Hall in London. The next day she had three reviews in the national papers. The first said she was a thrilling new star rising, the second that she gave a very nice and well-prepared recital, and the third that she should give up all hope of a professional career. She continued to work at the highest level for many years, so the third reviewer was wrong!

The days of the diva/divo who is indulged whatever her/his behaviour are long gone. Be a good colleague! 'Stars' don't really exist anymore and ego is not more important than talent and hard graft.

You may find that:

- You run out of energy to keep bouncing back after disappointment.
- You have to accept that you are not the standard required for professional work – this may be to do with stamina or giving consistently good performances. This is very hard to accept.
- The work that you are offered is not satisfying. You may prefer to give up rather than perform at a standard below the one you aspire to.
- New responsibilities – family ones for example – require you to have a more predictable and sustainable income than that of an itinerant musician!

However many people advise you, *you* will know when it is time to change direction. Trust your instinct on this.

Moving onwards and upwards

You may have to be patient before you can earn your entire living through singing. In the meantime, if you don't have private funds, deep-pocketed parents or rich and generous partners, you have to pay your bills. Many singers find that their performance skills and general propensity to communicate well make them favoured employees. You may even be able to dictate some of the terms of your employment, for example – what hours you work. Be aware of the fact that it is very hard to improve your singing if the sort of work you do is full-time, or vocally demanding – like telephone sales for instance.

If you have some flexibility with your working hours, then you may be able to fit in small one-off projects. Every singer learns best by doing performances. Whatever training you have had, and whatever studying you are continuing to do, you must try to keep performing. It may be more appropriate to aim at the fringes of the profession and gain stamina and experience rather than auditioning for big companies before you are ready. Consider anything that might enhance your performance, even if it is not paid. For example:

- Set up your own performances by organising concerts and recitals.
- Busk in approved locations.
- Sing with karaoke machines in pubs (but not smoky pubs!).
- Get together with a group of other singer friends and put on a concert. Include your favourite aria but also some duets and quartets.
- Sing in the chorus of a company that pays its principals but not its chorus – even singing in a chorus will be productive and you may be around excellent soloists from whom you can learn.

Try to have the mindset that you get your own work, rather than waiting helplessly for people to employ you. The idea that agents are out there ready to snap you up and sort out all your problems is actually a fiction!

Whatever happens with your aspirations to become a professional, try to keep on making music! Music enriches our lives and is endlessly surprising and fascinating. Singing connects you to your body and your soul. Working with musicians whom you respect and interacting with them on a musical plane – even without an audience – connects you to the music that inspires you.

Appendix

References for further information

Anderson, James	*Dictionary of Opera and Operetta* (Bloomsbury)
Brewer, Mike	*Warm-ups!* (Faber Music)
Chapman, Janice	*Singing and Teaching Singing:*
	A Holistic Approach to Classical Voice (Plural)
Green, Barry	*Inner Game of Music, The* (Pan)
Harnoncourt, Nikolaus	*Baroque Music Today: Music as Speech* (Amadeus Press)
Harris, Paul	*Improve your aural!* (Faber Music)(Grades 1, 2, 3, 4, 5)
Harris, Paul & Brewer, Mike	*Improve your sight singing!* (Faber Music)
	(Elementary – High/Medium Voice,
	Elementary – Low/Medium Voice,
	Intermediate – High/Medium Voice,
	Intermediate – Low/Medium Voice)
Hemsley, Thomas	*Singing and Imagination: A Human Approach to*
	a Great Musical Tradition (OUP)
Holden, Amanda (ed.)	*Penguin Concise Guide to Opera* (Penguin Books)
Hines, Jerome	*Great Singers on Great Singing* (Limelight Editions)
Johnson, Graham & Stokes, Richard	*French Song Companion, The* (OUP)
Jones, Kate	*Keeping your nerve!* (Faber Music)
King, Mary	*Singing In English* (High Voice) (Boosey & Hawkes)
Lascalles, George (Earl of Harewood) & Peattie, Antony (eds.)	
	New Kobbé's Opera Book, The (Ebury Press)
Legge, Anthony & Ford, Trevor	*Art of Auditioning, The* (Peters Edition)
Nichols, Roger (ed.)	*30 Italian Songs and Arias (17th-18th century)* (Peters Edition
Pegler, Heidi & Kemp, Nicola-Jane	*Language of Song, The* (Faber Music)
	(Elementary High Voice,
	Elementary Low Voice,
	Intermediate High Voice,
	Intermediate Low Voice)
Phillips, Lois	*Lieder Line By Line and Word for Word* (OUP)
Randel, Don Michael (ed.)	*New Harvard Dictionary of Music, The* (Harvard UP)
Stokes, Richard	*Book of Lieder, The* (Faber and Faber)
Stokes, Richard & Cockburn, Jacqueline (eds)	*Spanish Song Companion, The* (Scarecrow Press)

British Voice Association	www.british-voice-association.com